The True Meaning & Consequences of a Position of the Right Reverend the Lord Bishop of Bangor Concerning Sincerity, Asserted, Against his Lordship's General Charge of Misunderstanding

THE TRUE
Meaning & Consequences
OF A
POSITION
Of the Right Reverend the
LORD BISHOP of *BANGOR*
CONCERNING
SINCERITY,
ASSERTED,

Againſt his LORDSHIP's general Charge
of Miſunderſtanding, and the particular Exceptions of the Reverend Mr. *PYLE.*

Wherein is ſhewn,

That this Writer, inſtead of juſtifying his
LORDSHIP againſt the *Committee*, hath given
him up in every Particular.

WITH A
PREFACE,

Shewing by very plain Arguments, that his
LORDSHIP's Intention in writing his PRE-
SERVATIVE and SERMON, was to make way for
INDEPENDENCY.

By HENRY STEBBING, M. A.
Rector of Rickinghall *in* Suffolk, *and late
Fellow of St.* Catharines-Hall *in* Cambridge.

LONDON:
Printed for HENRY CLEMENTS, at the *Half Moon*
in St. *Paul's* Church-Yard, 1719.

THE
PREFACE.

THE following Sheets being entirely spent in the Proof of the most plain and obvious Things ; it must be wholly owing to the good Nature of my Reader if they meet with a kind Reception. I was from the very beginning conscious to my self how much the answering Mr. Pyle would want an Apology ; and even now I cannot see what Apology would be sufficient, should I trace him minutely thro' all his Objections, which (so far at least as they relate to the Points between his Lordship and the Committee) appear at first Sight to be purely the Effects of his own Uneasiness under Conviction, and his resolute Attachment to a desperate and indefensible Cause. Yet on the other hand to take no notice of any of them, I thought would be laying my self open to the Censure of his Lordship and his Friends ; whilst some perhaps would have look'd upon it as a silent Acknowledgment that I could not reply ; and others as an Instance of an indecent Contempt, that I would not reply to one, whose former Writings in this Controversy (if I mistake not) stand in the Catalogue of those whom even his Lordship himself has thought fit to appeal to, as (a) excellent Answers, and as coming from some of the ablest Hands that he knows of.

(a) *Answ,* to a late Book written by Dr. *Sherlock,* p. 111.

Under

Under this Difficulty one Expedient occurr'd, which I thought might be proper, viz. to set before the Reader a brief Specimen of this Gentleman's Way of Writing in one Instance, by which he might be able to judge of it in all the rest. And my Remarks *upon Sincerity being the shortest of all my* Tracts, *as a Defence of it might be managed at the smallest Expence, so I hoped that I should hereby entitle my self to so much* Candor *from the Publick, as not to have it thought, that if I pass by the other (as I fully purpose to do) it is because I have nothing to say; and that I should meet with so much* Justice, *as to have it acknowledged, that I am none of those who disdain every thing but what comes directly from his Lordship's own Hand. For my own part, as I am not a* Principal *in the Controversy now on foot, nor can presume to think my self of the Number of those* Persons of Weight, *whose Objections his Lordship hath somewhere promised to reply to at a convenient Season; so I cannot expect that his Lordship should ever particularly take notice of any thing that has been written by me. Nor indeed do I desire it; for I am not so unacquainted either with my* own, *or with his* Lordship's *Abilities, as not to be sensible how much the Truth may be in danger of suffering, if once her Cause should come to be tried upon so unequal a Foot. But tho' I may not expect to hear from his* Lordship, *yet surely I may hope that those who disapprove of my Writings, will either be wholly silent, or else that they will shew the Reasons of their Dislike in such a manner as is some way consistent with* Decency *and good* Sense; *and such Adversaries I shall never overlook, let them be who they will. But when* Men *write for no other Purpose than to vent their* Passions, *and rather than say* nothing, *are resolved to say any* thing; *their Answers are Answers to themselves, and not to me: So that if his Lordship should once more think fit to set forth Mr.* Pyle *as an* able Writer, *recommend his* Answers *to my Books*
as

as excellent Anſwers, *and expeſt that I ſhould be at leiſure to attend upon him as often as he ſhall be diſpoſed to call upon me, tho' I ſhall pay all that Deference to his Lordſhip's Judgment which ſuch a Caſe will admit of, yet (unleſs he very much mends his Hand) I ſhall think my ſelf obliged to have ſo much Regard to my ſelf, and to the Publick, as only to aſſure his Lordſhip that I can employ my Time to a better Purpoſe.*

But I fancy that by this time his Lordſhip himſelf is pretty well convinced, that it would be for his *Intereſt would this Gentleman leave his Defence to others, and try to ſerve him in a properer Way. For 'tis plain that the Service he hath hitherto done hath been,* not to *his Lordſhip, but* to the Committee, *of whoſe* Cenſure *there will be no room to complain, if that be his Lordſhip's Meaning, which Mr.* Pyle *has every where granted as ſuch. How true this is with reſpeſt to the Point of* Sincerity, *I have ſhewn at large in the enſuing Sheets; and how true it is likewiſe with reſpeſt to the main Point in debate, viz. the Point of* Church Authority, *it will be no hard matter to gueſs, from what I ſhall preſently obſerve to the Reader. 'Tis perfeſtly needleſs to examine particularly what Mr.* Pyle *hath objeſted to my* Remarks *upon that Head. His Obſervations are all of a piece with thoſe which I have here brought to the Trial; and had that part of his Book appeared by it ſelf, and without a Name, one might have judged by its Features to whom it belonged.*

But there is one thing which, had Mr. Pyle's *Obſervations been conceived under a more auſpicious* Planet, *would have made it not at all neceſſary for me to conſider them, which is, that his Lordſhip himſelf can, if he pleaſes, the moſt eaſily and effeſtually decide that Controverſy. The* Committee *have charged him with denying* ALL *Authority to the* Church. *My Buſineſs was to ſhew that they had reaſon to do it. This I did by a particular Examination of thoſe*

Passages upon which the Charge *of the* Committee *was grounded, which, according to the plain and obvious Sense of the Words, I have made appear to imply, that the Church hath* NO *Authority.* Now as the Meaning *of the* Committee *was not merely to censure his Lordship's* Words, *but the* Opinions *or* Doctrines *signified by those Words,* 'tis certain *that had his Lordship declared plainly that the Church has Authority, and shewn what that Authority is, the* Committee *would have accepted of such a Declaration as an Answer to their* Charge, *so far as it should have come up to an Acknowledgment of that Authority, which in their Opinion* ought to be claimed. *For the Question had then been not concerning his Lordship's Opinion, but concerning his Words only; not whether the Bishop judged right, but whether he had spoken right; which if he had not, it could have been of no Force against his* avowed Sense, *nor would have afforded any just Ground for farther* Censure. *Now that which would have satisfied the* Committee, 'ought also to satisfy me, and every Body else. And therefore I have declared in the Close of my* Remarks, *that* if his Lordship will fay that the Church HAS AUTHORITY; that there is a Power in some over others to prescribe Laws for Order and Decency in indifferent Matters in Religion, &c. I shall admit of his solemn Declaration against every thing that I have said; *i. e. I shall so far admit of it, as to think my self obliged not to enter into any farther Dispute with him upon this Matter. For as the reason why the* Committee *charged his Lordship with denying this Authority, was because they thought it to be* his Opinion *that there is no such Authority; so the reason of my defending that* Charge, *was because I thought so too. And therefore whenever the* contrary *shall appear, I shall think it will be far more decent in me to leave the World to judge, from what has already been offered, whether*

I had

I had reaſon *to think as I did, than to go about to juſtify my ſelf* anew ; *which indeed would be forſaking the* Subſtance *to hunt after the* Shadow, *and peſtering the World with a Diſpute of no manner of Uſe or Significancy.*

But it ſeems, to expeẟ that his Lordſhip ſhould declare himſelf upon this Point, is a very unreaſonable thing. (b) As if, *ſays Mr.* Pyle, it were HIS *(the Biſhop's)* Duty to ſet out all or any Boundaries of Power which a Church HAS, in a Diſcourſe profeſſedly deſigned for nothing elſe but defending ſincere Chriſtians againſt thoſe exorbitant Powers, which it manifeſtly has NOT ! *This was ſaid in anſwer to the Dean of* Chicheſter, *who in his* Preface *to my* Remarks *had obſerved,* (c) how carefully and reſolutely his Lordſhip had avoided declaring what one Branch of Authority he allows to the Church, inſiſting nevertheleſs that he had not denied ALL ; *and hereupon had taken occaſion to* call upon *him* by all the Regard that is due to Truth, to Religion, to the Goſpel, and to the Church of Chriſt, to ſay *it* without Diſguiſe. *To this Call of the* Dean, *I ſay, Mr.* Pyle *takes upon him to anſwer for the Biſhop, in the Words juſt now ſet down ; and he undertakes to juſtify this Anſwer by drawing* Parallels *more worthy of* himſelf, *than of his* ſacred Profeſſion *and* Character. This *(proceeds he)* is juſt as if I ſhould get an honeſt Man into my Houſe, and attempt to rob him, and then upon his defending himſelf and getting away, I ſhould indiẟ him at the next Aſſizes for ſtealing all my Goods and Chattels. ——*Again,* He *(the Dean)* has ſued and caſt me, ſuppoſe in a Matter of Encroachment upon Boundaries of Lands between us. Hence I conclude that he means to ſwallow ALL my Lands,

---

(b) Pref. to 3d Letter, p. 8, 9. (c) p. 3.

and

and leave me not a Foot or Furrow. Whose Business is it now, whose Concern to look out for
clear Titles, and to set out the several Abutments
and Boundaries of my Lands? *How well skilled
Mr.* Pyle *may be in the Methods of proceeding* in
Law, *I cannot tell; but I am sorry he has no better
Notion of that* Gospel *of which he is a* Minister, *than
to think that in* religious Controversies *Men are to
be governed by* the same, *and* no other *Rules, than
those which they are bound to observe in their Disputes about the* Abutments of Lands, *and in adjust-
ing Differences about* Goods and Chattels. *If one
Man prosecutes another only upon a* Suspicion *of*
Wrong, *the Law will allow him no Remedy; and the*
Defendant *having no Concern as a* Civil Subject *but
to clear himself* by Law, *'tis enough if the* Plaintiff
can make no Proof of any real Damage. *But what
is all this to the Purpose? Was his Lordship concerned
in this Case merely as a Civil Subject? Is he not to
be considered as a* Christian *and a* Bishop? *And was
it not his Duty under either of these Capacities,* to
have endeavoured by all possible means to take
away that Scandal, which, by his seeming *at least
to deny all Authority to the Church,* he had given to
Multitudes *of Men, if he had in earnest believed
that the Church has any Authority? I may presume
to ask this Question* now, *because I have* once before
asked it in vain; *and if Mr.* Pyle *be at a loss what
Answer to give to it, let him go to the* Gospel *and
learn what that means,* It is impossible but that Of-
fences will come, but wo unto him thro' whom
they come; *or that of the Apostle,* Let no Man put
a Stumbling-block or an Occasion of Falling in his
Brother's Way.

Mr. Pyle *may be pleased to put the Case in another
Instance, and try whether his* Divinity *will not help
him to a truer Sight of it than his* Law. *We will
suppose that some Man or other, eminent for his Learn-*
ing

...ng and Judgment, had given it out, that there is no *Sin* in *Swearing, and that Numbers of* others *should have been led to think that* any fort of *Swearing is* lawful, *and accordingly should have begun to allow themselves the Liberty of Swearing, fome* falfly, *fome* rafhly *and* vainly. *I put it to* Mr. Pyle *as a* Cafuift, *what would be an honeft Man's Duty in this Cafe? Would it be allowable in him to fit down and fay nothing? Or would it be enough for him to put it to* his Adverfaries, *to fhew that fuch Inferences could juftly be drawn from his Affertion? Ought he not rather, in the moft fpeedy and publick manner poffible, to* teftify *his* Abhorrence *of thefe wicked Profanations, and (to prevent fuch Abufes for the future) to* fet forth *particularly thofe Cafes in which* only *he meant to fay that* it *was* lawful *to* Swear? *I am perfuaded that there is no one, who has any Regard to the* Honour *of God, and the Salvation of Mens Souls, who will not think this Method to be juft and reafonable. And is it then nothing to God's Honour, nothing to Mens Salvation, whether that Authority which Chrift hath repofed in the Hands of his Minifters, be acknowledged and obeyed or not? Let* Mr. Pyle *either fhew this, or elfe let him fhew us a good reafon why the Bifhop, by whofe late Writings it is but too vifible that great Numbers have been led openly to infult and trample upon this Authority, fhould be exempted from the common Rules of Chriftianity (I may add, and of Humanity too) in like Cafes.*

There will be little need to obferve to my Reader, that the Argument goes all along upon the Suppofition, that the Bifhop does allow *that* there is *fuch an Authority; for if there be in his Opinion no* fuch *Authority, then in his Opinion there* will *be* no *Scandal* given *by leading* others *to think that there is* no fuch *Authority, and therefore* no *Scandal to be re-*moved. *I have faid thus much purely becaufe* Mr. Pyle *has forced me to it, by infifting upon it fo pofi-*

B *tively*

tively against Dr. Sherlock, who had called upon his Lordship to declare himself, (d) that he is not now obliged to do it by virtue of the Part he has hitherto acted in the present Controversy, altho' the Design of his whole Book is to shew that his Lordship hath not denied all Authority, but (e) such Authority only as is destructive of all real Religion and genuine Christianity. Against all such Authority as this I may venture to say, that we are as hearty Enemies as his Lordship, or the most zealous of his Friends. But this is not the Point: That which now lies before us is, Whether supposing that his Lordship allows of some Authority in the Church, he is not in Conscience obliged to set forth what that Authority is, in order to remove the Scandal which he has given to a great many, who have concluded from his Writings that he allows of no Authority. In proving that he is not, Mr. Pyle has put his Readers to the Expence of near Six Pages of Preface, the main Support of which has already been laid before you; the rest is fraught with such a Variety of groundless Conceits, and wicked Insinuations, as is hardly to be met with among any of the weakest and most profligate Writers of the Age. Having settled the Case of a Charge of THEFT falsly suggested, and that of a supposed Design of INCROACHMENT upon Lands, and determined what is to be expected from either Party, with the Gravity of a Judge in Westminster-Hall; at p. 10 he begins to grow merry; and considers how diverting it must be to the rest of Mankind, to see a Set of Men thus eagerly fencing and disputing about a certain Privilege and Authority, and yet all the while avoiding and shifting it upon each other to define what it is, and in whom it is lodged. At p. 12. he lets HIMSELF into the very Cause why the Dean

---

(d) Ibid. p. 13.   (e) Fourth Letter, p. 43, 44.

and

and some others are so loath to have any hand in
it, and why they so pathetically insist upon his
Lordship's performing this Part, *viz.* because there
may be great Hopes that HIS (*i. e. be Bishop*'s)
Openness, Sincerity, Plainness, and Undisguised-
ness, might happily bring THAT upon him, which
would finish the Dispute in favour of his Adversaries, sooner and better than all the Reasons they
can give, or the Pens they can ever employ against
him. *The* That *which stands here in Capitals refers
to* Temporal *or* Spiritual Authority, *mentioned in
the next Paragraph; so that according to Mr.* Pyle
the very Reason *why his Lordship is called upon to
declare what Authority he owns, is because it is hoped that such a Declaration would bring upon him* the
Censures of the Church (*and perhaps the* Secular
Power *too*) *as what will decide the Controversy much
better against him, than* Reason *and* Argument.
*One might be excused if he should infer from hence,
that in Mr.* Pyle's *own Opinion the Bishop has* such
*Notions concerning the Authority of the Church, as,
if he would plainly speak them out, would* subject him
to Ecclesiastical Censure; *which gives a fine Idea of
our* Ecclesiastical Laws, *when 'tis remembred that
the Bishop* denies no Authority, *but such* Authority as is destructive of all real Religion and genuine Christianity. *To exclaim against* all *such* Censures *in the gross, he learn'd from the Bishop himself;
and whoever does it, 'tis a* Symptom *which to me as
surely* indicates *an* inward Disposition *to* innovate
in the Church, as a Man's calling out to have all Civil Courts *of* Judicature *abolished, would shew his
Intention to* overturn *the* State. *But let this be as
it will, thus much is plain, that those, whoever they
be, who either have called, or shall hereafter call upon
his Lordship to* explain himself, *are represented as
Persons conscious to themselves that their Cause cannot
be maintained upon the Foot of* Reason, *and yet resol-*
B 2 *ved,*

ved, if they can, to fupport it merely by the Dint of Authority. *A few Lines after their Character is compleated, and they are declared to be* Adverfaries, whofe Hopes are the fame with thofe of the JEWS, in their captious Queftions put to our Saviour, that upon either fide of the Determination there might be Stones enough ready to caft at him. *This is a fine Comparifon! But the* Calumny *is too grofs to be fupported by fo weak and flender a Foundation. To call upon his Lordfhip to tell us what Authority* he owns, *and what* he denies, *is highly reafonable, if it were only upon this Account,* viz. *that we may no longer continue fighting in the Dark, without knowing what it is neceffary for us to prove. The Authority claimed by us is, as we judge, the very fame with, and no other than, that which our* Church *has claimed ever fince the* Reformation. *His Lordfhip cannot be ignorant of thefe Claims; and therefore if he knows of any in which he thinks either that* we *have departed from* our Church, *or* our Church *from the* Scriptures, *let him fhew which they are, and he fhall have a fair hearing. But till this is done, to expect that* we *fhould undertake to defend any* particular Claim *againft his Lordfhip, is ridiculous; becaufe whatever Claim we fix upon, his Lordfhip, when all is done, may tell us that he never oppofed this Claim, and fo it muft be left entirely to his Lordfhip's Difcretion to determine to the* World, *whether we have not been very* impertinent. *How far this would be our Cafe if we fhould go about to defend* all our Claims, *it is impoffible to fay with any manner of Certainty; for his Lordfhip by declaring that he hath not denied* all Authority, *and yet refufing to tell us what Authority* he owns, *has left himfelf at Liberty to own juft as* much or as little *as he fhall think fit; fo that if we fhould make good every thing which we pretend to (for we do not pretend to* all Authority) *we cannot be certain but that his Lordfhip may make ufe of his Liberty otherwife*
                                                    than

than we expect, and declare for it too ; the true Con-
sequence of which is, that the more able we are to de-
fend and justify our selves,   the more danger we are
in of saying a great deal to very little Purpose. Whe-
ther this be putting things upon a fair Bottom, let
any one judge.   To me this Cautious *Way of Deal-*
ing seems to betray much more of Craft *and* Policy,
than of true Courage   *'Tis just as if I should use*
all the Means I could to provoke a Man to Fight
me, and when I find him ready, should sneak off, and
leave him to try his Strength upon some Body else,
that so I might the better know whether I am able to
Encounter him   Whether this be his Lordship's *Case,*
he himself best knows, but I cannot forbear saying it
looks somewhat like it.   In writing his Preservative
and Sermon, *he was thought by all the Friends of*
the Established Church *to have proclaimed* open
War *against her ; and his drawing back so soon af-*
ter the Alarm was taken, and pretending that he
was only Arguing against the Papists, *and I know*
not who, seems to have been only an Umbrage to shift
the Cause into other Hands ; that so he might secure
to himself the Benefit of a Retreat, in case the
Success should not answer his Expectation   If
this be so, it will then be the Concern of his Friends
to call upon him to declare *; by whom he has not dealt*
so kindly as they deserve, if after having put his
Hand to the Plough, *which is to tear up the Foun-*
dations of our Establishment, he looks back *and*
leaves them to bear the heat and burden of the day.
But if not, and his Lordship shall still insist upon his
old Plea, that he has not denied all *Authority, it*
behoves us, I think, to call upon him, not as Mr Pyle
weakly supposes, to deliver us out the Particulars of our Authority (*for we want not to be in-*
structed in what we pretend to) but deliver out to us
the Particulars of his own, *i. e. of that which he*
                                                    will

*will stand by ; and if it shall appear to us to be less
than what we think may be claimed by the Gospel, it
will soon be seen whether we will shift off the Cause
from one to the other, as if it were too hot to be
meddled with, or whether it may be* better *supported
by* mere Authority, *and* Human Engines, *than
by the solid and lasting* Foundations *of* Judgment
and Reason

But if his Lordship will not be prevailed upon to
declare himself for our sakes, he ought certainly to do
it for the sake of others, even Multitudes of Men to
whom he has done infinite Wrong, if there be any
one Branch of Authority which he allows to the
Church. The thing is too plain to be denyed, and I
doubt not but his Lordship sees it as well as I I could
indeed have no good Opinion of his Lordship, had I no
other way of finding out his Character, than from
Mr Pyle's Writings : But even he, with all his In-
discretion, shall never provoke me to think that this
Right Reverend Prelate is either so weak a Man as
not to know, or so bad a Man as not to consider,
that the Ministring to others an Occasion of depar-
ting from the Faith of the Gospel, is a thing of which
some account will be required another Day To do it
with Design, is one of the highest Affronts we can
offer to God ; and what is undesignedly done, becomes designed, if afterward we do not endeavour,
to the utmost of our Power, to repair the Injury. And
what then can be expected from his Lordship, whose
fertile Labours have so plentifully Administred to the
growth of Libertinism among us, and produced so
many rude Attacks upon the Church and Clergy ;
what less, I say, can be expected from him, than
that he himself should with his own Hands apply
a Remedy to these Evils, by asserting those Rightful
Powers (whatever they be) which chiefly thro' his
Means have been set at nought ? That so his Lordship's Great Name and Character may not hence forward*

w.ird be made to Patronize those very Opinions which he himself disallows of; that the Enemies of our Church may no longer claim him as their own; nor Deists and Free-Thinkers continue to Caress and Compliment him in vain.

If Mr. Pyle can shew that there is nothing in all this, he is at full liberty to do it, and then, and not before, he may perhaps be able to calumniate those, who shall call upon his Lordship to explain himself, with a better Grace. But as for his Lordship, I will not, I cannot mistrust him so far as to think he will attempt it. He knows himself to be a Debtor to the Wise, and to the Unwise, and to have to do, (tho' Mr. Pyle (f) seems to imagine that none but the Committee have) with the Brethren at large, the Weak as well as the Strong. He knows full well what Influence the Eminency of his Station, and the Credit and Reputation he has obtained in the World, has in determining the Sentiments of others agreeably to his own ; and upon this account must think himself bound by the Regard he owes to that Gospel, of which he is an Ambassador, to that Church of which he is a Bishop, and to all those Christians who have been Witnesses of his Conduct in this Particular, if indeed he does own any Authority, to declare plainly what it is. Of all these things, I say, I make no doubt but that his Lordship is truly sensible; and therefore his studied Reservedness in this Case ever was, and ever will be a strong Argument with me, that the Charge of the Committee is not to be Refuted. I omit to mention those Reasons, which in Point of Prudence might move his Lordship to such a Declaration. Of his own Private Affairs he himself must be allowed to be the best Judge; tho'

(f) *Fourth Letter*, p. 83.

I

I should hope that no Private Views *would so far have prevailed over him, as to lead him to the Neglect of so* Publick *and so* Necessary *a* Duty. *But there is one thing which I must not forget to mention, viz* His Lordship's *great* Tenderness *of his own* Character, *which of late has appeared in a very remarkable Instance. It is not long since his Lordship was charged with having* Prevaricated *in a most Solemn Appeal to Almighty God. A heavy, and (as I believe) a very groundless Imputation it was; and his Lordship, as it behoved him, left no* Stone *unturned to remove it. But to leave this Point to be decided in* Books, *was not thought safe; the* Remedy *might be too* slow *for the Disease; and therefore* Advertisements *thronged upon* Advertisements, *and every* News Paper *groaned under the Burden of the Controversy. How adviseable this Method was, I shall not take upon me to determine; but this I say, that when I consider his Lordship's* Zeal *in the one Case, and his* Coldness *in the other, I cannot in* Charity *so much as suspect that he owns any* Authority. *For if I did, the Inference would force it self too strongly upon me, viz. That his Lordship has a much greater* Concern *for his own* Honour, *than he has for the Honour of his* Lord *and* Master.

The Reader I hope will forgive me, that I have detained him so long upon this Point, *when he considers that I am all this while endeavouring to show, that there is at present no necessity for me to enter upon a particular Defence of my* First Treatise. *I shall now offer one Argument more, which tho' I dare not call a* Demonstration *in the strict Sense of the Word, yet, I may venture to say, is sufficient to satisfy any reasonable Man, that it* never *will be necessary. I do assure his Lordship, and the World, that I speak it with no manner of Delight, or Complacency; but with the deepest Concern; for I rate*

not the Peace *of the* Church *fo low in my Efteem,
nor am fo little fenfible how much it may be in his
Lordfhip's Power to difturb it, that I had not infi-
nitely rather find my felf miftaken with the* Committee *in judging of his Lordfhip's Senfe, than find
him miftaken in a Matter of fuch Confequence as this.
But if any Regard is to be paid to what the Writers
of his Lordfhip's Side have openly and conftantly
maintained, it will appear, that whenever his Lordfhip fhall declare himfelf (if he fhall at any time think
fit to declare himfelf) it will be abundantly to our
Juftification; there being not fo much as one of thefe
(fo far as I have feen) who has not denied* all Authority *in the Church in as full Terms as poffible;
and advanced fuch (I will not fay* new Schemes; *for
indeed they are only the* old independent Notions
*revived; but fuch Schemes) as are utterly inconfiftent
with all* Order *and* Government. *To fet this
Matter in a clear Light may not be improper, in
order to clofe up this Controverfy, which has now
been almoft* Two Years *on foot, concerning the* true
Intent *and* Meaning *of the* Bifhop's *Sermon: I
fhall difpatch it as briefly as I can.*

It is to be obferved then, that when we fay the
Church *has Authority, our Meaning is, that there
are* certain particular Perfons *in the Church who
are vefted with Authority from* Chrift. *This Authority is fuppofed to be both* Legiflative *and* Judicial. Legiflative, *as thefe Perfons are authorized
to make* Appointments *about* indifferent Matters
relating to Order *and* Decency *in Religion and the
Worfhip of God; which* Appointments, *under proper Circumftances, fhall be* binding *upon the* Confciences *of others* And Judicial, *as they are em-
powered to determine upon what* Terms *and* Conditions Men fhall be *admitted to, or excluded
from,* external *and* vifible Communion. *Who thofe*

C   *Perfons*

Persons are who are entrusted with this Authority,
it is not at present needful to enquire; tho' 'tis very
obvious to gather, and it has been generally so un-
derstood, that if there be such an Authority, it must
originally *have been lodged in the Hands of the*
Clergy. *But this can be no Part of the Question*
with those who deny that there is any such Authority
any where at all; and that this is the Case of those
who have appeared in Defence of the Bishop *of*
Bangor, *I am now to shew   I shall confine my En-*
quiries to the first *Branch of* Authority *only, viz.*
the Authority *of* Legislation; *for when this is once*
destroyed, the other must fall of course.

The Reader perhaps will be surprized to see Mr.
Pyle *standing at the Head of those who have denied*
all *Authority, if he considers in how angry a manner*
he has treated me, for endeavouring to shew that the
Bishop *has denied* all *Authority.   But when he*
grows to be a little acquainted with him, he will
learn to wonder at nothing of this Kind; for he will
find it to be his constant Practice, *under the Pretence*
of writing for *the* Bishop, *to write* against *the* Bishop *and* himself *too.   A few plain Passages out of*
his fourth Letter *will set this Point out of the way*
of Exception.

(g) We say then *(says* he*)* that the Church
(mean by it what you will) needs not at all be
supposed to derive its Authority of appointing
indifferent Things from any express CHARTER or
DELEGATION from Christ —— we find no such
determinate COMMISSION or Privilege DELEGA-
TED to the Church, nor was there occasion for
it.   *Here is a plain Declaration that Christ has gi-*
ven no special Commission *to the Church to* ap-

(g) P 65.

point

point indifferent Things ; *now if this be true, then he can have given no Special Commiffion to any particular Perfons in the Church. This is granted in exprefs Terms.* (*h*) The chief Texts, *fays he,* whereon is pretended to be built an exprefs COMMISSION from Chrift to PARTICULAR PERSONS as CHURCH GOVERNOURS, have been confidered by the Bifhop and his Advocates, and fhewn to have no relation to fuch Kind of Power, *&c. And therefore he declares a few Lines after, that the reafon of our* OBEYING *fuch (for fo he fpeaks, tho' very improperly) is not becaufe of any exprefs* CHARTER given them BY CHRIST, as RELIGIOUS or SPIRITUAL GOVERNOURS, to make Appointments in indifferent Matters. *Again,* (*i*) *The chief Miftake lies in imagining that Mens Obedience is due to it (*i. e. *to a* Church *Law*) *by virtue of a pofitive* COMMISSION *given by Chrift to* CERTAIN MEN *as* SPIRITUAL RULERS. *And* (*k*) *elfewhere fpeaking of* Spiritual Powers *by* DERIVATION *from* Chrift *to certain* PARTICULAR PERSONS, *he fays they are* DREAMS. *The Author of a Pamphlet under the Name of* Phileleutherus Cantabrigienfis, *treads in the fame Path.* (*l*) It does not (*fays he*) any where appear that God has given the Power of making Laws or Rules about the Circumftances of his Worfhip and Service, to any PARTICULAR PERSONS among Chriftians: therefore no Perfons have a DIVINE RIGHT to this Power. *And this Notion is alfo fupported by Mr.* Burnet, *who fays of the* Clergy *in particular, that* (*m*) they are appointed ONLY to TEACH, to EXHORT, and to ASSIST others in the

---

(*h*) p. 67. (*i*) p. 69. (*k*) p. 88. (*l*) Effay on impofing Articles, p 7. (*m*) Second Letter to Mr. *Law,* p. 198, 302.

Performance of their Duties. *That they have* *properly any* Authority *he (n)* denies; for this, *says he,* implies Command and Dominion, which St. *Peter* exprefly forbids Paftors to exercife. *And* *he says of* all *Chriftians, without Exception, that they* (o) are all equal, and upon a foot; *and that none* *of them* (p) have a Power of making Laws, fo as to bind the Confciences *of others.*

It appears then from what thefe Gentlemen do una- *nimoufly teach, that there are* no particular Perfons in *the Church to whom Chrift has granted a* Power *or* Commiffion *to* make Laws *for* Order *and* De-cency; *the Confequence of which is manifeftly this,* *that there is in the Church* no Legiflative Authori-ty. *For a* Legiflative Authority *implying, in the* *very Notion of it, a* Power *of* making Laws, *which,* *under proper Circumftances, fhall be* obligatory *upon* others *(for otherwife they are no* Laws) *'tis plain,* *that if there be any fuch Authority in the Church, it* *muft be lodged in the Hands of* fome particular Per-fons in *the Church. It is plain alfo that thefe* par-ticular Perfons *muft have received this Authority* by a Commiffion *from* Chrift; *becaufe Chrift being* *the* Head *and* fupreme Governour *of the Church,* *whatever Authority there is in the Church, it muft* *have been* granted by *or* derived from *him. But* *why do I labour to deduce that by way of Confequence,* *which thefe Gentlemen do fo liberally grant me of their* *own accord?* Mr. Burnet *you fee confeffes the Charge,* *and tells us, that no* fallible Men have a Power of making Laws in Chrift's Kingdom, fo as to bind the Confciences of his Subjects. Mr. Pyle *goes* *farther a great deal;* (q) There CANNOT *(fays he)* IN THE NATURE OF THE THING be a proper Human

---

(n) Ibid. p 154.   (o) Ibid. p. 55.   (p) Ibid. p. 263.
(q) Ibid p. 71.

LEGISLATIVE

LEGISLATIVE Power at all, even in the EXTERNALS
of Religion, as there is in Civil Affairs. *This sure-*
ly is a Stretch beyond all Reason! For what? Could
not Christ, if he had so pleased, *have given a* Power *to* some particular Persons *to make* Laws *rela-*
ting to the external Modes *or* Circumstances *of Re-*
'ligion? Why no it seems; and the Reasons are, be-
cause there can be no Power to which the Subjects
can be ABSOLUTELY and CONSTANTLY obliged, or
which can rightly and really PUNISH for Non-
compliance. *Worthily argued! As if* Punishment,
i. e. Temporal *Punishment, were of the* Essence *of a*
Law! *Or as if* Power *must either be* absolute *or*
none at all! *If this be true, it will as well follow that*
there can be no Human Legislative Power *in* Civil
Affairs. *For I know not where that* Civil Power *is,*
which can oblige the Subjects absolutely *and* constantly, *or* under all Circumstances

But it is not my Business at this time to dispute
whether there be *in the Church any proper* legislative
Authority, but only to enquire whether these Gentle-
men do allow *that there is; and it is, I think, as*
plain as Words can make it, that they do not. *'Tis*
true they very frequently use the Word Authority,
and speak of Church Governours, Church Laws,
and the like; but in this they only use a Latitude of
Expression, which may serve to impose upon careless
Readers; for when you come to examine precisely in-
to their Notion of Authority, *&c. it is manifest that*
they intend no such Matters as those Words and
Phrases do properly *imply. This will be more evi-*
dent still, if you consider what Account they give of
the Ground *and* Foundation *of* Church Communion, *which, says my Author,* Mr. Pyle, (r) *is of an*
Human, Social, *and* Civil Nature. (s) The Church,

(r) Ibid. p. 66. (s) Ibid. p. 65.

he

he tells us, cannot but be fuppofed to have an Authority of appointing indifferent Things, as it is a Society, and by virtue of its very Nature of being fuch ; and therefore it is both impowered and obliged to keep up that Order and Regularity, which in the Courfe of Reafon, Nature and Providence, is neceffary to and obligatory upon all Societies. *There are two or three Paragraphs more full of fuch Stuff as this ; by which thofe who are well verfed in* Unintelligibles *perhaps may receive fome Edification. But thofe who love plain Words, I muſt defire to attend me to the next Chapter, where we ſhall find a* Key *which will let us into the whole* Myſtery. *I had in my* Remarks, p. 80. *taken notice of the Biſhop's way of interpreting the* 20th Article *of our* Church , *wherein it is declared that* the Church hath Power to decree Rites and Ceremonies. *His Lordſhip's Senſe of the Matter is this : That ſince the* Church (*in the preceding* Article) *is defined to be a* Congregation, &c. *therefore whatever is here affirmed of* the Church, *muſt be ſuppoſed to be affirmed not of* any particular Perſons, *but of* the whole Congregation. Is not this (*ſaid I*) taking away all Authority in fome Chriftians above others to prefcribe Laws for the external Manner of religious Worſhip ? *Why yes, ſays Mr.* Pyle, (*t*) juſt as much as for any CIVIL Body of Men to agree upon Laws for preferving Society, would be taking away all Power of fome over others ; but no more. For neither the one nor the other, by fuppofing the Power of Law-making to be lodged originally in the WHOLE BODY, carries any Denial but that the Power of executing their Laws may be delegated to PARTICULAR HANDS. *How much this Anſwer is to the Purpoſe,*

(†) Ibid. p. 86.

will

will be seen anon ; thus much is plain at the very first Sight, that according to Mr. Pyle, Church Communion, *i. e. the joining of many Persons together in one particular* external Way *or* Manner *of religious* Worship, *is founded not in any* Power *or* Authority *which is* originally *lodged in* some *above* others *of* prescribing *or* appointing *that* Manner, *but in the* Consent *or* Agreement *of the* whole Body *or* Congregation *so joining together ; which appears yet farther from what he says a little after,* viz. (*u*) That when any Church or Society of Christians have appointed Ceremonial Usages for the sake of common Decency in Worship, those Members, &c. *Now as this is entirely agreeable to what the Bishop supposes to be the Sense of the Article, so it answers to the Notion which is constantly and unanimously maintained by the Writers aforementioned.* Mr. Burnet *perpetually speaks of the* (*w*) Agreement *of Christians, as the Foundation of* external Order *in the* Church. Phileleutherus Cantabrigiensis *tells us plainly, that* (*x*) the only Foundation or Right any Form of Church Polity can be settled upon, is the Consent and Appointment of the Christians who unite into that Church ; *and* that Consent is the only Foundation of Ecclesiastical as well as of Civil Government. *Once more then I ask the Question;* Is not this taking away all Authority *in one* Christian *above another to prescribe Laws for the* external Manner *of* religious Worship; *or, which is the same thing,* can *there upon this Supposition be any* such thing *in the* Church *as a* proper Legislative Authority? *In answer to this Question, it is granted in the first place, that* one Christian has not ori-

---

(*u*) Ibid. p. 88.   (*w*) Ibid. p. 131, 132, 133, 134.
(*x*) Ibid. p 7, 8.

ginally

ginally *a Power of prescribing Laws* over others *in
these Cases* ; *for Mr.* Pyle *tells us, that* ORIGINALLY
the Power of making, *i. e. of appointing* Rites and
Ceremonies, is in the WHOLE BODY. *Well ; but
may not the* whole Body DELEGATE *this Power into
some* particular Hands, *whose* Appointments *about*
indifferent Things *shall, in virtue of that* DELE-
GATION, *acquire the* Nature *and* Force *of* Laws?
If this may *be, altho' the Difference will still be very
great between us, yet it must be owned that there*
may *be in the Church a* proper LEGISLATIVE AU-
THORITY ; *and this is what Mr.* Pyle *seems to insinuate by his putting, in the way of Comparison,* Ecclesiastical *and* Civil *Societies upon the same Bottom. His Supposition is, that* originally *all Men are*
equal, *as well with respect to their* Religious *as their*
Civil *Concerns : and his Argument is to this effect ;
that to say that the* Power *of appointing* Rites *or*
Ceremonies *for the Preservation of* Order *and* Decency *in religious Worship, is lodged originally in the*
whole Body, *no more takes away* all *Authority in*
one CHRISTIAN *above* another, *than to say that the*
Power *of appointing* Laws *for the Preservation of*
Society *is originally lodged in the* whole Body,
takes away all *Authority of* one CIVIL SUBJECT
above another ; because neither of these Suppositions
carry with it any Denial, but that the Power——
may be delegated to PARTICULAR HANDS. *This
seems manifestly designed to insinuate a Belief into
his Readers, that there are some* particular Persons
in the Church *who have a proper* legislative *Authority* delegated *to them from* the whole Body, *even
as (according to these Mens Politicks at least) there
are in* the State ; *and certainly it was necessary for
him to say this, or else, as is manifest, and as I
suppose he himself saw, his Answer will have no relation to my Question. But it is evident also, that
in Truth he intended to say no such thing ; for when*

you

you come to look what that Power *is which he pretends may be* delegated *from the* whole Body, *it is not what the Comparison would naturally lead you to expect, a* Power *of* MAKING Laws, *but a* Power *of* EXECUTING Laws *already made,* i. e. *it is not a legislative, but an* executive *Authority. What* Chicanerie, *what* Legerdemain *is this! It is not for* SUCH *Management, I hope, that* Mr. Pyle *has so decently complimented his Lordship with being the Author of a new Sect, and so frequently in his Writings stiled himself* A BANGORIAN.

What this Power *of* executing *Laws, when applied to* the Church, *can possibly mean, I shall not for my Part so much as pretend to conjecture. 'Tis enough for me that* Mr. Pyle *does not here say that* the Body *of* Christians *can* delegate *to any* particular Hands *a proper* legislative *Authority; and I am certain he cannot say this without contradicting what he has before advanced in general,* viz. *that* there cannot in the nature of the thing be a proper Human legislative Power at all, even in the Externals of Religion, as there is in Civil Affairs. *In truth, such a* delegated *Authority as this there cannot be in the Church without an* express Commission, *or at least without an* express Permission *from* Christ; *the reason is plain,* viz. *That tho' Men may give up their* Natural and Temporal *Rights into what Hands, and upon what Terms they please, yet they cannot give up their* Religious *and* Spiritual. *In the Use and Exercise of the* former *they are indebted to* none; *but in the Use and Exercise of the* latter *they are indebted to* God. *So that if it be supposed that* Christ *hath* originally *left all Persons at liberty to worship God in such a Way and Manner as they themselves shall best approve of,* i. e. *if he has* not *himself subjected them to any as* Lawgivers, *they* cannot subject *themselves to any as* Lawgivers, *without affronting him. Wherefore I say, in order to*

D   *make*

make way for a proper legislative *Authority upon this foot, it must be shewn from Scripture that Christ hath permitted Christians to* delegate *that* Power or Right, *which* originally *is lodged in* all *of them* equally, *to* particular Hands, *and by them to be* governed *and* directed *as* Lawgivers *in Matters left undetermined by him*; which should any one attempt to do, he would attempt something which is not only impossible, but very ridiculous. For it is upon many Accounts more reasonable to suppose, that if Christ had intended that Christians should be subject to *particular* Persons *as* Lawgivers *in this* Case, he himself would have appointed *those* Lawgivers, *rather than have left them to* appoint *them* for themselves ——— But there is no need for me to insist any longer upon this, which indeed is Nobodys Notion that I know of, but only a mere Suggestion of Mr. Pyle's, to get rid of an Objection which he could not answer. My Question was this, viz. Whether supposing that the Right of appointing Rites and Ceremonies was not lodged in the Hands of particular Persons in the Church, but in the whole Congregation, as the Bishop had asserted, it would not necessarily follow that there was no Authority in one Christian above another to appoint these Rites, and consequently no Authority in the Church at all. Mr. Pyle saw how this pinch'd, and found that the Objection could not be removed without saying, that tho' this Power was in the whole Body, yet it might be delegated by the whole Body to particular Hands. Now to have asserted this plainly, and without Disguise, would have been grosly to have contradicted his own declared Sense; and not to assert it, was clearly to give up the Point. This was worse than Death; and therefore he chose the middle way, i. e. to seem to assert it, and yet not to assert it; a Practice which is I confess worthy of such Writers as value the Credit of a Party more than they value the Truth;

Truth; *but can have its desired Effect only upon such*
Readers *as trust to their* Ears *more than to their*
Understandings.

The Result of the whole is this; *that according to
these Men there is no such thing as any proper* legiflative *Authority in the Church of Christ*; *but that
all* Christians *are at liberty, notwithstanding any* Pre-
eminence *or* Superiority *which Christ hath given to*
one *above* another *(which they do not grant) to join
together* (any Number of them) *in the use of such*
outward Forms *of religious Worship as they themselves shall most approve of.* I say, any Number of
them; *for if* Consent *be the* only Foundation *of*
Ecclesiastical Polity, *as these Men exprefly contend,
it will follow, that if a Man does* not consent *to any
particular* Form *of* Ecclesiastical Polity, *he cannot
be* bound *to that* Form, *nor any longer bound than he
is* consenting; *that is to say, he is perfectly at liberty
(notwithstanding any Obligation which the* Consent
or Appointment *of* others *can lay upon them) to
join in* that Form, *or* any other *which he likes better.
Men can* consent *only* for themselves; *and to say
that the* Consent *of any Number of Christians in* one
Way *of* Worship, *binds* others *to join in the* same
Way, *is to plead for that* legislative *Authority which
they difown. For whatever it be by which a Man is*
bound, *that is a* Law, *and* Authority *will be* Authority *let it be lodged in the* Hands *of* many, *of a*
few, *or of* one. *Wherefore, I say, when thefe Au-
thors fpeak of* Ecclesiastical Authority *or* Ecclesiastical Laws, *they abufe the Words, and their Readers too. For by* Authority *they can mean only a*
Right *or* Power *relating to* themselves only; *and by*
Laws *they can intend nothing but certain* Rules *or*
Orders, *which by the mutual* Consent *or* Agreement
of Christians have been settled among themfelves.
Mr. Burnet *himfelf in effect confeffes thus much. For*

says

says he (*y*) when any vifible Church or Congrega-
tion of Chriftians have (NOT MADE a Chriftian
LAW, for that they have NO POWER to do, but)
AGREED upon any particular ORDER for their own
Edification ; it is then a Sin (not againft any LAW
made by that AGREEMENT, for SUCH there can be
NONE properly fpeaking ; but) againft the great
Law of Peace and Charity to leave that Order,
without fome very weighty Reafons. *I ſhall make
a farther Uſe of this Paſſage by and by* ; *what I produce it for at this time is, to ſhew, that according to
Mr.* Burnet, *the* Orders *or* Appointments *of Chriſtians about the* external Manner *of* religious Worſhip, *are not properly* Laws ; *and that the* Obligation *not to depart from any* ſettled Order *without
good reaſon, ariſes not from hence, that Men are*
bound by *that* Order, *but from the* general Law *of*
Peace *and* Charity ; *by which it is plain Men are
oft-times bound, even in the moſt* indifferent *Matters.*

    *And now I will beg Leave to ask his Lordſhip one
plain Queſtion. Will he ſtand by theſe Doctrines, or
will he not ? If he will not, why, in the Name of God,
has he not long before now ſhewn his Diſlike of them ?
Why has he not remonſtrated againſt theſe either miſtaken or deſigning Men, who have appeared under
the Character of* Interpreters *and* Defenders *of his
Writings, and told the World plainly that they have
not repreſented his Meaning truly ? But alas ! his
Lordſhip has given the World too much reaſon to
think, that theſe Gentlemen have fathom'd to the
very bottom of his* Schemes ; *and that what they*
ſpeak, they ſpeak not of themſelves ; *Mr.* Burnet
eſpecially, whoſe Second Letter *his Lordſhip hath*
(z) *ſet forth in ſuch a manner, that one cannot but*

(*y*) Ibid. p. 131.   (z) Anfw. to Dr. *Sherlock*, p. 111.

                                 ſuſpect

suspect that he was no Stranger to the Contents of it before it was published. And if this be the Case, it might perhaps be worth his while to consider, how he will be able to justify his late Conduct to God, and to the World. For these are the very Doctrines which were charged upon him by the Committee; *which Charge his Lordship hath not only denied, but hath taken occasion from hence to represent the* Commitee *as Setters up of the* Popish Claims *of* absolute Authority *and* indispensable Obedience; *whereas it is plain to the Eyes of every one who is but willing to see, that the* Charge *carries no such Meaning, nor any other Meaning than that, in which his Lordship, if he would have spoke plainly, must have confessed the Justice of it. It would be easy for me, by the help of this* Clue, *which I have now put into the Reader's Hand, to lead him thro' all the* Labyrinths *of his* Sermon, *and his* Answer *to the* Representation, *and shew by what a Variety of artificial Turns he has endeavoured to perplex and confound his Readers. But as it was never any Part of my Design to render his Lordship odious, but only to justify those whom he had render'd so, I shall here stop my Hand, and leave the rest to those who are more fond of such Work than I am. I take no Delight in gazing upon the Frailties of my Brethren and Fellow Christians; and as to his Lordship, I do assure him I am so far from being desirous of saying any thing amiss of him, that I am for his sake, as well as for the sake of* others, *sorry that he has given me the occasion to say what I have said. If this therefore be (as I trust it is) enough for those whose just Cause I have been pleading, it shall be enough for me; nor shall I so far divest my self of my Humanity, nor shew my self so inconsistent in my Professions of a Concern for the Honour of our most excellent Church, as needlesly to expose those Faults of a Bishop of her own, which should her Enemies (as at some time or other perhaps*

*haps they may) caft in her Teeth, fhe muft be for-
ced to turn away her Face with no other Reply
than this,*

———— Pudet hæc opprobria nobis
Et dici potuiffe & non potuiffe refelli.

*One thing I have now to offer to thofe Gentle-
men, whofe Writings I have juft been looking into;
which I offer, not fo much as an Argument againft the
Truth of their Principles (for it is not my Bufinefs at this time to decide that Point) but principally to lay open to them the* full Extent of them,
and fhew that they infer a Conclufion, *of which
I believe they are not ferfible, and of which when
they are once made fenfible, they may perhaps think
it neceffary to examine them over again.* Mr.
Burnet *has told us in the Place laft quoted,
That* when any vifible Church or Congregation of Chriftians have ———— agreed upon any
particular Order for their own Edification ; it
is then a Sin ———— againft the great Law of
Peace and Charity to leave that Order, and
make other new ones, without very weighty
Reafons. *The Cafe you fee relates to* external
Communion ; *and to avoid multiplying Queftions,
I fhall fuppofe the meaning of the Paffage to be
this - That when the Chriftians of any* Nation,
or the major part *of them, have agreed upon any
particular* Order, *i e. upon any particular* Form
of Ecclefiaftical Polity, *it is then a Sin in any
Perfons of that* Nation *to forfake, or not to con-
fent to that Form, but to fet up others of their
own, without fome weighty Reafons.* Mr. Burnet
*will not be difpleafed, I hope, that I fuppofe him
to be a* Friend *to* National Churches, *and that
I take his Defign in this place to have been, to
guard againft* needlefs Separations *from that particular*

ticular National Church *of which he is a Member.
If he be, I ask his Pardon; but if I may have leave
to interpret* him *by* Phileleutherus, *I judge right;
for he tells us, that* (a) every one is under an
Obligation to unite with that Form he finds
ready settled to his hand, provided —— (*I need
not repeat the Conditions) and adds:* A Man who
lives in a NATIONAL CHURCH, is obliged to unite
with THAT. *This Gentleman you see pleads for a*
National Church; *and he pleads for it so far as
to tell us elsewhere (tho' for what reason I profess I
cannot see) that* (b) to imagine that in a Christian Nation there should be no National Church,
is UTOPIANISM *By a* National Church *he means
(or I cannot tell what he means) some* particular
Form *of* external Polity, *which the* major part
of the Christians in a Nation have consented to.
For all Ecclesiastical Polity *being (as we are now
taught to believe) founded, not in any* Laws *of* particular Persons *appointing a* particular Form, *but
in the* Consent *of Christians;* a National Church
therefore cannot receive its Denomination *from such*
Laws, *but from* Consent; *and if from* Consent,
it must be from the Consent of the Majority. *For
if there can be no* National Church, *unless every
single Christian of a Nation shall* agree *in the*
same Form, *to imagine that there* can be *any*
National Church *at all will,* I doubt, *be* Utopianism. *And besides, a* National Church *upon
this Supposition will be utterly inconsistent with a*
Separation; *because it must cease to be a* National Church *as soon as there is a* Separation.
We will suppose this then to be the Case; and

(a) Ibid. p. 9.   (b) Ibid. p. 17.

say

fay with Mr. Burnet, *that it is a Sin against the Law of* Peace *and* Charity *to* feparate *from a* National Church *without fome* weighty Reafon. *The Queftion that I would ask is this ;* What may be adjudged a weighty Reafon *in this Cafe ? Mr.* Burnet *anfwers in the very next Words, that it is* fuch a Reafon as drives *Men* to the Choice whether they will adhere to CHRIST or to MEN ; *or fuch a one at leaft,* in their fincere Opinions. *This I confefs is fomewhat loofely expreffed ; but we may explain it by fome other Paffages. He tells us then elfewhere, that* (c) It may often be commendable to fubmit to Terms and Conditions which it was very unlawful to impofe, where thofe Terms do not DIRECTLY OPPOSE the END of all EXTERNAL COMMUNION. *And again in another Place* (d) His Lordfhip, *fays he,* in a Difpute that he was engaged in with the DISSENTERS —— only endeavours to prove —— that the Terms of Communion which they fcruple, are not IN THEMSELVES UNLAWFUL. *I doubt not but that Mr.* Burnet *approves of this Argument of his Lordfhip ; and therefore from all this I gather, that, according to him, it is a Sin for any Man to feparate from a* National Church, *unlefs the* Terms of Communion *impofed by that Church are, or appear to them to be,* in themfelves unlawful, *i. e. unlefs that Church requires fomething be performed of its Members which Chrift has particularly forbidden.* Phileleutherus *fays the fame thing.* (e) Where (*fays he*) there is a NATIONAL CHURCH which is BARELY TOLERABLE, *i. e.* in the Conftitution of which

(c) Ibid. p. 241.   (d) Ibid. p. 278.   (e) Ibid. p. 18.

there

there are ever so many Errors, Defects, or
Corruptions, yet if NOTHING SINFUL is imposed on, or required of the Members of it, 'tis
the Duty of all the Christians in that Nation
to hold Communion in that Church; *and af-*
ter this he also refers to some of the former Wri-
tings of the Bishop of Bangor, *from whence he*
has produced a long Passage which is to the
same Effect.

The Case then is thus far clear, that to forsake a
National Church, *and join to another, is* a Sin;
if the Terms of Communion *imposed in that Na-*
tional Church *be simply lawful; which tho' I ac-*
knowledge to be a very great Truth, yet I cannot see
how it can be defended upon these Men's Principles.
For the Sin *of Separation is by them supposed to*
consist, not in the Breach of any particular Law *by*
which in this Case Men are bound to communicate
with the National Church *(for such a Law, in*
their Opinion, there cannot be) but in the Breach
of the general Law *of* Peace *and* Charity. *That*
is to say, notwithstanding every Man with respect to
any particular Law *which others have Authority*
to lay upon him, is perfectly at Liberty to join in
Communion *with any* Church *or* Congregation *of*
Christians, *yet the* general Law *of* Peace *and*
Charity RESTRAINS *him in the use of that* Liberty,
and makes it necessary for him to communicate with
the National Church. *The Case appears to me to*
be exactly the same with that which is mentioned
and resolved by St. Paul, *concerning the* eating of
Meats *in themselves* indifferent. *There is no par-*
ticular Law *of* God *which forbids me the use of*
any sort of Meat *any more than another, and con-*
sequently, with respect to any such Law, *I am*

E   *perfectly*

perfectly at liberty to eat *of* any. *But yet if any one be offended by my* eating *of some one particular sort, I am obliged to abstain from it, by that* general Law *of* Charity *which forbids me to* offend *my* Brother.

This you see is the sole Foundation upon which these Men build the Sinfulness *of separating from a* National Church; *a Foundation, in my Opinion, by much too weak to bear the Weight of such a Superstructure To make which evident, I lay it down as a general Rule, that the Law of* Peace *and* Charity *can have no place but in things* merely indifferent *to the great End of Man, i e. to his* Final *and* Everlasting Happiness. *Of this sort are all those things which relate to the* Body; *for which neither Reason nor Religion binds us to make the* best *Provision we can, and therefore we not only may, but oftimes ought to forego many Conveniencies of this kind, for the good of others, and especially for their spiritual good. But certainly both Reason and Religion oblige every one of us to make the* best *Provision we can for our* Souls, *and therefore I am not to forego any one Advantage of this sort for the sake of others; for this were to suppose that in a matter of the greatest Consequence I am obliged to prefer the Interest of* others before *my own. Although therefore if any one be offended, i e be betrayed into Sin by my* eating *of some particular sort of* Meat, *I am by the Law of* Charity *bound to abstain from that sort of* Meat; *yet if any one should be offended at my* praying *so many times a Day, or at my* fasting *so many Days in the Week, I should (if I found any real spiritual Advantage by those Exercises) be so far from being obliged to* forbear *them, that on the other hand I*

should

should be obliged to continue *them, notwithstanding such* Offence. *For that such a Person is* offended *is* his own *Fault, and 'tis unreasonable that I should debar my self of any* spiritual Good, *merely to gratify anothers* Frowardness.

To apply now this general Rule *to the* Case *before 'tis. We will suppose a* National Church *already constituted, the* Terms of Communion *in which are only* simply lawful, *or (as* Phileleutherus *speaks from the Bishop of* Bangor *himself)* barely tolerable ; *since all things that are* lawful *are not equally* expedient, *it must be supposed that* other *Forms may be contrived, which will contribute* more *to the* spiritual Improvement *of Christians. Put the* Case *then that a certain* Number of Christians, *sensible of this, should have* agreed upon, *and constituted another* Form *among themselves really* more beneficial ; *and then ask any one of these* Gentlemen, *what they will have to say to shew the* Reasonableness *of complying with the* National Form *To urge barely that the* National Form *may lawfully be complyed with, is nothing to the* Purpose, *for these* Persons *are supposed to have separated, not upon the* Account *of any unlawful* Terms of Communion *imposed upon them, but only upon the account of* greater Expediency *If it should be said that Separations from a* lawful National Church *give* Offence, *i e become the* Occasion *of* Hatred and Strife *among Christians, and argued from the* general Law *of* Peace and Charity *that they ought to conform ; the* Separatists *may answer ;* " Look ye to that, who are *unchari-* " table *and* contentious ; *we bear a* Good Will " *towards all* Men, *and are desirous to live peacea-* " bly *and* quietly *with you, and every one of those* " *who do, or shall, differ from us. That ye have*

" no

" *no* Authority *by any* Law *of yours, to* bind *us*
" *to* your Form, *ye confess; and why then should ye*
" *be* offended *at us for making use of that* Liberty
" *which Christ has given us for our* Edification ?
" *We cannot answer it to God or our own Con-*
" *sciences, to neglect any Opportunity he has put*
" *into our Hands for our spiritual Improvement;*
" *and therefore we cannot depart from* our Form
" *to join in* yours, *which we are satisfied does*
" *not so well promote and set forward the great*
" *Ends of* Religion. *We acknowledge our selves*
" *bound by the* Law *of* Peace *and* Charity; *but*
" *we think that this Law will not reach our Case.*
" *We are ready to consider the Frailties of our Bre-*
" *thren, and shall take care to avoid every thing*
" *which may minister unto them an Occasion of*
" *offending God,* so far *as is consistent with our*
" *own* Eternal *Interest. But if you expect that*
" *we should sacrifice any part of our Share in*
" *God's Favour to the Passions and Prejudices of*
" *others, you impose upon us a very unreasonable*
" *Task, and we do not think our selves bound to*
" *comply with it."* What reasonable Answer could
be given to such a Plea as this, I must profess
for my own part, I am not able to see. If these
Gentlemen can think of any themselves, I should be
glad to hear it.

I need not observe, that the Argument will be
the same, whether you suppose the Form agreed upon
by this separate Congregation, to be really better
than the National Form, or only so in their Opinions. For in truth, that is most expedient to me
which I my self judge and find to be so. Right
and Wrong have their fix'd Limits, which are not
to be alter'd by the Opinions of Men. But in
judging

judging of the Usefulness *and* Expediency *of any thing, regard must be had to Men's* Circumstances, Tempers, *and* Dispositions ; *and consequently that which is* in general *and in the main most expedient, may not be so to* every particular Person. *Now if the Reader should be in pain lest these* Separatists *should want* Ministers *to officiate in their Congregations, Mr.* Burnet *will very quickly relieve him. For as to* administring the Sacraments (f) *one* Christian *has as much Right to do it as another, tho' the whole Congregation may, if they think so fit, order it to be performed by him whom they shall appoint* to be their Mouth ; *i. e. by the* Minister ; *for you must know* Ministers *are only the Mouths of the People ;* (g) *God has not appointed any particular Order of Men to* preach *and* officiate *in* Holy Things, *but hath left every Body or Congregation of Christians to* appoint *them for themselves. This is the goodly Fabrick which is now rearing up upon my Lord Bishop of* Bangor's *Shoulders ! Which if it can be supported, all Disputes about* Separation *will be at an End. For it will then be lawful for* any Set or Number of Christians *in* any Nation *to disjoint themselves from the* National Church, *to appoint* Pastors *of their own, to settle* Rules *and* Orders *for God's Worship* among themselves, *if at any time the* National Forms *should happen not to be to their own liking. If these* Gentlemen *can shew that this Consequence will not follow from their Principles, it concerns them to do it ; if not (and I am perswaded they cannot) it should be a means to give them at*

(f) Ibid. p 165, 166, 167.

(g) Ibid. p. 43. 57. 154 163. 168. 198. 118, 119.

least

leaft fome Diftruft *of themfelves, and to bring them back to a more impartial Search after that much defpifed* Authority *of fome over others, which alone can adminifter a Remedy to this Evil. For certainly if there be no* Medium *between* Popifh Tyranny *and* Slavery *on the one hand, and an* unreftrained Licentioufnefs *on the other; or (which is the fame thing) if the Gofpel allows of none; the State of Chriftianity is very much to be lamented;* God *will not be, as he has declared himfelf to be, the* Author of Peace, *but the Author* of Confufion; *nor will the* Church *of* Chrift *agree with thofe* orderly *and* œconomical *Reprefentations by which it is defcribed to us in the Holy Scriptures.*

By this time I think it is but too manifeft what was the true Defign of the Bifhop of Bangor's *Sermon and* Prefervative; *or if there be any who can yet doubt, they muft feek Satisfaction from fome other hand; for to me this part of the Controverfy feems fo fully determined, that I fhall never trouble my felf any farther about it. I have faid thus much* now *in order to poffefs the Reader with a juft Senfe of the Importance of the Debate that is likely to enfue. To fhew him that the Difpute is not concerning any nice Points of Speculation, about which Chriftians may fafely differ among themfelves, but about a matter which muft neceffarily affect the* Peace *and* good Order *of the* Church *The Caufe is manifeftly to be pleaded over again between the* Church of England *and* Independency, *only with this difference, that whereas the Debate was formerly ufed to be managed by the* Church of England *againft* avowed Separatifts, *or the* Enemies *of all* Religion *(who delight, at every turn, to throw in fomething, as a Bone of Contention among us) it is now to be*

managed

managed by the Church of England *againſt ſome of her own* Communion, *yea, what is more, againſt ſome of* her own Miniſters, *with a* Bishop *of her own at the Head of them* This is an unhappy Circumſtance I confeſs———But ſince it muſt be ſo, I may venture to promiſe it will *be ſo, being well aſſured that among ſo many Learned and Judicious Divines which now adorn our Church, there will not be wanting thoſe who wi'l exert themſelves in a Cauſe upon which* Her Safety, *and by conſequence the* Honour of Jeſus Chriſt, *and his moſt Holy* Religion *does ſo much depend*

I have run this Preface *out farther than I expected; and to a Size, I fear, very diſproportionate to the* Treatiſe *which it introduces. But if the Reader has met with any thing in it which he thinks worthy his Obſervation, he will not be diſpleaſed that I have detained him ſo long; for to deal ingenuouſly with him, 'tis more than I dare promiſe he will find in the* Book *itſelf.*

A
DEFENCE
OF THE
Remarks upon SINCERITY, &c.

CHAP. I.

Containing some Observations upon his Lordship's general Censure of that Book.

IN the Lord Bishop of *Bangor's Answer to the Dean of* Chichester's *Vindication of the Corporation and* Test *Acts*, Chap. 2. Sect. 8. p. 117. I find this Account given by his Lordship of my *Remarks upon a Position* of his *concerning Religious Sincerity*, viz. That therein I have *bestowed* a great deal of *Severity and Satyr upon an incidental Sentence of his; the grammatical Sense of which I have greatly mistaken, and from the real meaning of which I cannot suffer my self to differ one Hair's Breadth.* A few Observations upon these words, will serve as a very proper Introduction to what is to follow afterwards. And

First. His Lordship, you see, is pleased to call that *Position* of his upon which I have remarked, *an incidental Sentence;* at which I must confess I

B   ma

am very much furprized For an *Incidental* Sentence, in the Language of every body, fignifies
a *Sentence* which is brought into any Difcourfe
by Accident ; or, in other words, a *Sentence*
which has no *immediate Relation* to the *main Point*
under Confideration. Now then either his Lordfhip muft allow us to fay, that *all* he has faid
about *Sincerity* is *incidental*, or he muft not pretend that *this Sentence is incidental* If the Reader has his Lordfhip's *Prefervative* at hand, I defire he would turn to *p.* 85. There he will find it
laid down in general, that the thing which *jufti-*
fied the *Proteftants* in their Separation from the
Church of *Rome,* was their *being perfwaded in their*
own Confciences that the Popifh Doctrines and Wor-
fhip were corrupt. At *p* 86. this Doctrine is applyed to the Cafe of *Papifts* and *Nonjurors* ;
There alfo it is declared to be *a certain Rule to*
go by in all like cafes, and confequently that as
the *Private perfwafion* of the *Nonjurors* will juftify them in their Separation from the *Papifts,* fo
the *Private Perfwafions* of any other Chriftians
will juftify them in their Separation from the
Nonjurors. Thus far therefore his Lordfhip had
been teaching in effect, that a Man's *Private Per-*
fwafion will juftify him in the Choice of *any*
Communion, be it in its own Nature what it
will Now at *p.* 89. comes the *Demonftration*
which was brought to prove all this, and which
by this time, I fuppofe, is fo well known, that I
need not repeat it. I fhall only add, that at
p. 91 his Lordfhip fums up this whole Difcourfe
in one fingle and general Inference (which is the
very *Propofition* upon which I made my Remarks)
The Favour of God THEREFORE *follows Sincerity*
confidered as fuch, and confequently equally follows
every equal degree of Sincerity.

This

This is the Truth of the Case; and now let any unprejudiced Person judge between us, whether this be an *incidental* Sentence or not.---- But what signifies it, perhaps you'll ask, to consider this? Why truly not much as to the merits of the Cause. For if his Lordship has *incidentally* said that which in its Consequences will *certainly* and *necessarily* evacuate all the Laws of the Gospel, considered as available to the Salvation of Men; his Lordship, I think, ought to be told of it, and desired for the future to be more careful in what he writes. But that which I Remark this for, is to shew you that I have *not* (as his Lordship by this Pretence would insinuate that I have) laid *greater stress* upon this Sentence than he himself appears to have laid upon it; but on the contrary, that I chose it for the Subject of my *Remarks*, as it was a Passage in which the whole Substance of his Lordship's Doctrine about *Sincerity* was briefly comprimized, and consequently a Passage from whence of all others we might the most certainly judge, how much his Lordship intended to conclude from those Arguments which he had made use of in the foregoing Parts of the Discourse But were it so that I had taken that Advantage which it appears I have not taken, how indecently does his Lordship complain of it! To say a Thing *happen'd by chance,* is in some sort offering to *excuse* it; which can never be consistently done, unless there be also an acknowledgment of *something amiss.* But his Lordship in effect declares, that in this *Sentence* there is *nothing amiss.* He tells me, that I have put a wrong Construction upon his words, and sends me back to my *Grammar* to find out the right One. To observe now after this, that it is an *Incidental Sentence,* and insinuate from hence that I have treated it with *more severity* than I ought, can serve to no purpose; unless his Lordship had a mind to set forth his own *Abilities,* by shewing that even the most careless Passages in his Books, are such as will stand their ground against the *severest* and most critical Examination.

But I must not pretend to take this amiss from his Lordship, since he has treated a much greater Man than my self after the same manner , I mean the Reverend the *Dean* of *Chichester,* who is charged with (*a*) *Popular Address,* because in the *Title Page* of his Book he *has undertaken to write a Vindication of the* Corporation *and* Test Acts, *in Answer to* HIS *Reasons for the Repeal of these Acts.* His Lordship has so mortal an Aversion to *Popularity,* that I question not but that he looks upon the least step towards it to be criminal, especially in the *Dean;* and thus far I am willing to agree with him, that to do a Thing *merely* for the sake of *Popular Applause,* is beneath a Man of Sense, as the endeavouring to compass it by base and little Arts is unworthy a Man of Honesty. Now if it be of any concern to the Publick, whether the *Corporation* and *Test* Acts be Repealed or not Repealed, the *Dean* I trust may be thought to have had this at heart, when he wrote his *Vindication,* and consequently he will be acquitted of the Charge of affecting Popularity on the first Score And how he can be charged with it on the other Account, it would, I believe, puzzle the most cunning Man upon Earth, except his Lordship, to find out. For what ? Has the *Dean* attempted to make himself Popular at his Lordships expence ? Has he written a *Vindication* of the *Corporation* and

---

(*a*) Answer to the Dean of *Chichester,* p. 3.

Test

Test Acts, *in Answer* to his Lordship's *Reasons* for
the Repeal of those Acts, which *Reasons* his
Lordship *never gave?* Why no His Lordship has
given *Reasons* for Repealing these Acts; but the
Case is this, *which all who are too much prejudiced
to read on both Sides will not be led to judge,* viz.
That these Reasons are only a FEW WORDS ACCIDEN-
TALLY DROPT *in the Body of another large Debate.*
Very good; and his Lordship should have
been forgiven this *Mischance,* if he would have
retracted these *Reasons* ; but so far is it from this,
that this Plea stands in the Front of another
large Debate, wherein his Lordship *ex professo,*
and with all his might labours to *justify* these
Reasons! Was ever any thing in the World so
pleasant as this! His Lordship seems to be of
Opinion, that 'tis wrong to Animadvert upon
any Thing that HE says, unless he thinks fit to
write a *great Book* about it! Let his Notions be
never so false in themselves; let them end in the
Ruin of *Christianity* or of *Civil Government,* or
of *both*; yet if he does not draw them forth in
their full length by a Treatise on purpose, but
drops them in *few words* here and there, as it
were *by accident,* in the Body of some other
large Debate, all is well on his Lordship's Side,
and 'tis as much as a Man's Reputation is worth
to go about to meddle with him! If his Lordship can make it out very plainly by what right
He claims such a Priviledge as this, I make no
doubt but he will find his Account in it But
if not, all this will appear to be only a kind Endeavour to load an Adversary with more than
falls to his share; and then I suppose it will
very quickly be seen who it is that *affects Popularity.*

I beg the *Dean's* pardon that I have intruded
thus far into his Province; The Case is so exactly

ly parallel to mine, that I could not forbear taking this Notice of it ; And I muſt needs acknowledge that 'tis ſome ſmall comfort to me to
find, that I am *the leaſt* of thoſe whom his Lordſhip has thought fit to deal with in this trifling
manner.——— But I muſt proceed no farther upon
this Point, for fear of giving his Loidſhip farther
Diſpleaſure. For when all is done, *this* may be
ſaid to be *an Incidental Sentence* as well as the
other, and I may expect to be told of it if I
ſhould handle it *too roughly*. Wherefore

Secondly This Sentence (whether *incidental* or
not incidental, for I care not now which you call
it ; this Sentence I ſay) it ſeems I have not rightly underſtood. *The grammatical Senſe of it I have
greatly miſtaken, and from the real meaning of it I
cannot ſuffer my ſelf to differ one Hairs breadth.*
Now if by *the real meaning of this Sentence* his
Lordſhip underſtands *that which* HE *really meant*
by this Sentence, I anſwer, that I am not at all
concerned to inquire whether I differ from it, or
differ from it not. A Man's *meaning* is to be
judged of from what he *ſays* ; and therefore if
his Lordſhip has ſaid *one* Thing and meant *another*, the Conſequence of that muſt lye upon
himſelf, and not upon me. The only thing
therefore to be conſidered is, whether I have, as
his Lordſhip ſays, miſtaken *the Grammatical Senſe*
of this Sentence, *i e*. Whether I have affixed
any other Senſe to this Sentence, than what the
words according to the moſt plain and obvious
conſtruction do naturally import This I ſay is
the Point, which I ſhall firſt Debate with his
Lordſhip ; and after that I will diſcuſs ſome
other matters in my Book which have been
excepted againſt. Give me leave only, before I
proceed, to make this one Obſervation, *viz.*
That his Lordſhip by alledging that I have *miſ-*
taken

taken the Senfe of his Pofition, has tacitly owned that in the Senfe I have put upon it, it cannot be defended ; which I hope may have fome
weight with thofe who underftanding his Lordfhip as I have underftood him, do yet pretend
to juftify him in what he has there advanced.

CHAP. II.

Containing an Anfwer to Mr. Pyle's *Exceptions againft my Interpretation of his Lordfhip's* Pofition.

MY *Remarks* upon *Sincerity* may be divided
into *three* Parts The *Firft* is that in
which I have endeavoured to ftate the Senfe of
that *Pofition* in his Lordfhip's *Prefervative*, which
is the *Subject* of thofe *Remarks*. The *Second* is
that wherein I have laid down *the Confequences* of
the *Doctrine* contained in that *Pofition*. The
Third is that in which I have confidered *what
foundation* that Doctrine has *in the Nature and
Reafon of things*. Concerning the *Firft* of thefe
the Queftion now is, whether I have ftated the
fenfe of that *Pofition* rightly, *i. e.* according to
the moft natural and obvious import of the
Words, or not His Lordfhip, you fee, has
declared his Opinion on the Negative fide, tho'
he has not been pleafed to give any Reafon for
it, or to tell me whereabouts my Miftake lies.
Whether he ever intends to do it I cannot tell ;
but if he does intend it, I hope to fpare him
the trouble, by fhewing that the Words are not
truly capable of *any other* Senfe than that which
I have put upon them. And becaufe Mr *Pyle*
is

is the only Perfon that has particularly confider'd what has been offered by me upon
this Branch of the Controverfy, I fhall therefore be obliged to make him the Principal in
this Debate   Only I muft let this worthy Gentleman know aforehand, that I think it neither
needful, nor proper, to perfue him ftep by ftep,
but that I fhall take in his Exceptions as they lie
in my way, according to that Order and Method, which I judge to be moft convenient.

The Pofition then (if it needs to be repeated)
is this ; *The Favour of God follows* SINCERITY,
*confidered as fuch, and confequently equally follows
every equal Degree of* SINCERITY.   Concerning the
Senfe of the word *Sincerity*, I am fure I fhall
have no Difpute with his Lordfhip or his Friends.
Mr. *Pyle* can tell me with a fneer, that I have (*b*)
acknowleged *his Lordfhip's Definition* to be *very
juft.*   And fince this Gentleman fets out upon
the merry Pin, I'll give him leave to laugh at
me once more, by telling him that perhaps I
was a little too hafty in making this acknowledgment *Sincerity,* according to his Lordfhip, is
(as I faid) when a Man follows the Dictates of
his own Confcience or Underftanding, after
having made ufe of the beft *means* he has, for
his *Information.*   But *Sincerity* in common Speech
(I think) is ufually oppofed to *Hypocrify*, and
confequently implies no more than that a Man
acts according to his *real Sentiments,* whether he
has ufed the *beft means* for his *Information,* or
ufed them *not* Mr *Pyle* himfelf has ufed the
word in this Senfe (*Letter* p. 28.) where fpeaking of St. *Paul,* who declared he had *lived in all*

(*b*) Third Letter to a Member of the Univerfity, *p.* 4.

good

goodConfcience; he declares the meaning of it to be, that *he was* SINCERE, *or void of* DOUBLE DEALING. However, I do not in the leaft repent me of this Conceffion. The World was even then well nigh tir'd out with this Controverfy, and I was therefore willing to make my part in it as fhort as I could. Wherefore feeing his Lord-fhip had fo plainly told us what HE meant by *Sincerity*, and feeing every Man has a right to ufe words in what Senfe he pleafes, provided he takes care to acquaint his Reader how he ufes them : I thought it better to follow his Lordfhip in his own way, than to ftand cavilling with him about his Definition ; upon which Account I did not fo exactly confider whether it was right, or whether it was wrong. If his Lordfhip there-fore will pardon the Injury, I will once more leave this matter as I find it, and proceed to the words *confidered as fuch* Now by Sincerity *confi-dered as fuch*, (I faid) his Lordfhip means Since-rity *of it felf*, or Sincerity *alone* ; and Mr. *Pyle* is fo kind as to (c) *agree with me* in this, *if by the Phrafes* OF IT SELF *and* ALONE *I mean——* If? Why do you doubt, Sir? my words are plain, if you are but willing to underftand. By Since-rity *of it felf*, or *alone*, I mean, and can mean nothing elfe than Sincerity, without any other *Circumftance* or *Qualification*. And this is what his Lordfhip means by Sincerity *as fuch*, or he means nothing. 'Tis ridiculous therefore in you to fay, that you *will agree with me, if by Sincerity alone, I mean Sincerity without the Obfervance of any thing claimed by the Authority of other Men as neceffary to Juftification*. For Sincerity without any other *Qualification* excludes every thing you

---

(c) Ibid.

C

can

can conceive, as well as thofe Things, *the obfer-vance whereof is claimed by the Authority of Men.* But what does his Lordfhip mean, when he fays, That the Favour of God *follows* Sincerity? Why this too I have explained, and fhown it from his Lordfhip's own exprefs words, to be, that Sincerity gives a Man a *Right* or *Title* to God's Favour. This left no room for Hefitation, and therefore I have Mr *Pyle* confenting to it freely, and in as full Terms as I could wifh. This, fays he, (d) *is true in all that Latitude wherein* Man *can be underftood to have any* Claim *or* Title *upon* God, *either with refpect to the Reafon of Things, or to any exprefs Promife from God.*

Thus far therefore Mr. *Pyle* himfelf could fee that (e) *there would be but very little difference between us.* I will venture to fay, that thus far there *poffibly can be no* difference between us upon any juft and reafonable Ground. The only Difpute, fo far as I can perceive, will lie in this, *viz.* What is the true import of thefe Words, *equally follows every equal Degree of Sincerity.* Now for the clearing up of this Point in my Remarks, I offered it to be confidered, that in *Sincerity* there are *no Degrees.* Hereupon Mr. *Pyle* very gravely asks: (f) *Does the Gentleman mean no Degrees of one Man's Sincerity above that of another; or no Degrees of it in one and the fame Man at different times? or does he intend to be underftood as denying it in both Inftances——?* But why all this Queftioning again? Every one fees, that when I fay that there are *no Degrees in Sincerity,* I mean (what only can be meant) that *Sincerity* is one, *fimple, indivifible* Thing, which admits of neither *more* nor *lefs,* and confequently that I *muft*

(d) Ibid. (e) Ibid, (f) Ibid.

be underſtood as *denying* that there are *Degrees* of *Sincerity* in ALL Inſtances where *Sincerity* comes under Conſideration But *this,* that there are *no degrees* of *Sincerity,* I did not ſet down as *(g) his Lordſhip's meaning;* i e as if *his Lordſhip had ſuppoſed,* that there were *no Degrees* in *Since-rity,* as Mr. *Pyle* very idly and extravagantly ſuggeſts; No; but I offered it (in direct *oppoſit-ion* to his Lordſhip, who *ſuppoſed* the *contrary*) as that which neceſſarily reſulted from the very No-tion of *Sincerity,* which being (according to his own Definition) then, and then only, when a man uſes *his* BEST *Endeavours,* it muſt therefore lie in an *indiviſible Point,* and conſequently be either *wholly* or *not at all.* And this I did, that I might at once ſhew the true and full Extent of his Lordſhip's Principle, which being, that all Perſons *equally ſincere,* are *entitled* to *God's Fa-vour*; it muſt therefore (if there be *no Degrees* of *Sincerity*) be affirmed *abſolutely,* that ALL *Sincere Perſons* are *equally intitled* to *God's Favour.*

I know not whether it will be worth my while to conſider this Point over again; becauſe upon ſuppoſition that Sincerity *will admit* of *Degrees,* his Lordſhip's Principle will be liable to the very ſame Objections, as I ſhall ſhew you by by. However, becauſe Mr. *Pyle* has been very elaborate upon this Argument, that he may not grow too big in his Triumphs, I will briefly re-ply to his grand Objection, which is this, *viz.* (h) That *the word* BEST is oft-times uſed *in a Re-lative or Comparative Senſe.* That *Sincerity* can-not imply *the doing* EVERY THING, *and uſing* EVERY MEANS *that comes within the ſtrict poſſibility of a Man's Power,* becauſe if it does, *no Man* perhaps

either is, or ever was Sincere. Confequently
that the Bifhop in defining *Sincerity* by a
Man's *ufing his* BEST *Endeavours, cannot be fuppofed* to have ufed that Phrafe in that *Rigid* and *Un-
limited* Signification.—— Thus in effect, Mr.
Pyle. But to what purpofe, or for whofe ufe is
this? For mine? I have no occafion for *fuch*
Inftructions; I never was fo Abfurd as to imagine
that Sincerity *does* imply the doing *every Thing,*
and ufing *every means* that comes within *the ftrict
poffibility* of a Man's Power. I never fuppofed
that by a Man's *ufing his* BEST *endeavours* his
Lordfhip meant any Thing elfe, or that any
Thing elfe can in found Senfe be meant, than a
Man's ufing *all thofe means* which either *do,* or
may appear to him to be *reafonable* and *fitting.*
And therefore if this be what Mr. *Pyle* would
have when he fays, (1) That *by God's requiring a
Man's utmoft Endeavours in the ufe of all proper
Means, is meant nothing more than his requiring of
him all thofe Things or Means which the Perfon
knows and feels to be plain and eafy for him to underftand, and are fairly within the compafs of his
Power and Faculties to attain :* If this, I fay, be
what he intends by *this* and fome other fuch like
loofe and *undeterminate* Sentences, by which he
has defcribed to us the Nature of *Sincerity,* I
fhall have no Difference with him on this Account.
But what will he get by all this? Let him try if
he pleafes, and fee whether *this* Notion of *Sincerity* will not exclude *Degrees,* as much as if it
were fuppofed to confift in doing *every Thing*
that comes within the *ftrict poffibility* of a Man's
Power. To me it is as plain as any Thing can
be that *it does.* For if *Sincerity* confifts in a

(1) Ibid. *p.* 6.

Man's

Man's ufing ALL thofe Means which do or may appear to him to be reafonable and fitting, it is evident that he who falls fhort of this, is not *at all* Sincere. Suppofe then that he has gone *thus far;* Can he go any *farther?* Can he? Yes, without doubt, in the Notion of *ftrict poffibility,* he can; But in the way of *good Senfe* and *Reafon* he cannot. He may *do* more, but he cannot be *more Sincere;* For to do *more* than what is *reafonable* and *fitting,* is not *Sincerity* but *Folly.* There can be no Queftion but that Mr. *Pyle* might, if he pleafed, travel into *France* or *Italy,* and learn the Doctrines of *Popery* from the Mouths of fome of the moft celebrated *Profeffors.* But fhould he Attempt this notwithftanding, upon the moft mature deliberation with himfelf, he was fully convinced that he might *as well* fatisfy himfelf about thofe Doctrines by their *Writings at home,* he might applaud his own Induftry if he would, but for my own part I fhould think that his time might be much better employed.

If Mr. *Pyle* will be pleafed to confider of this, he may fee perhaps at the laft, that I am not fo much out of the way in affirming, that there are *no Degrees* in *Sincerity.* Nor let me be any more told that (*k*) *there are Degrees of* ACTIVITY *and* INDUSTRY *in the ufe of means and opportunities of Knowledge.* As yet I have Senfe enough left to fee that this is *true,* and at the fame time to difcover that it is nothing at all to the Purpofe. If indeed *any* Degree of *Induftry* and *Activity* were Sincerity, (*i. e.* if *Induftry* and *Sincerity* were *all one*) then I grant, *that Sincerity muft have Degrees.* But forasmuch as this is not the Cafe, but *Sincerity,* even according to Mr *PYLE's* own Notion (if he has any determinate Notion at all about it) *then only* is, when a Man

(*k*) Ibid.

is arrived to the *last* and *highest* Degree of *Indu-stry*, which it is *reasonable* and *fitting* for a Man to use; let him consider, I say, once more of what I have said, and make out his *Degrees* as well as he can—— But enough, and too much upon a Point which does not enter into the Essence of the Debate. For, as I observed just now, which way soever the Case be determined, his Lordship's Principle will be liable to the same Objections. The main Fault I find with it (as every one knows) is, that it makes God, in dispensing his Favours, to have *no regard* to *any Thing but the Sincerity of Mens Hearts*; which if it be true, will be *equally* so, whether *Sincerity* has *Degrees*, or whether it has *none*.

To set this Matter aside, therefore; and to come to something which Mr. *Pyle* seems to be not a little angry that he did not hear of before. He tells his Friend, That (*l*) *the next Thing naturally to have been expected from me, in order to have compleatly stated the Sense of his Lordship's Proposition, was to have defined what is meant by the* FAVOUR *of God, and what by its following Sincerity* EQUALLY And here he charges me with great *Reservedness* and Secrecy, in *not opening at first Entrance the plain and simple Meaning of these Words*, but *bringing it in as Turns should serve*, for the sake of I know not what After-game which I had to play, and of *drawing* certain *Conclusions* and *deadly Inferences* from *strenuous Premises.* Now I beseech you, Sir, by the love of Truth, to hear me with some Patience. I do freely and ingenuously confess, That I have neither *at first Entrance*, nor *any where* in my Book, set my self *professedly* to explain these Phrases; but from the

(*l*) Ibid.

bottom

bottom of my Heart I do assure you, That I
had no such *Plots* and *Contrivances* in my head
as you are pleased to fancy, nor was there any
other Reason for my omitting this, but only
that I could not in the least suspect that these
Phrases *needed* any explication. By the *Favour
of God*, every one understands (if indeed any
words there be by which it can be made plainer)
the *good Will*, or *Approbation* of God, together
with all those *Benefits*, or *Blessings*, which he be-
stows in consequence of that *Approbation* ; and
Mr. *Pyle* was so very sensible of this, that although he has found Fault with *me* for not explaining this word, yet *he himself* has not so
much as once explained it, but proceeded all
along in his Argument *upon this* Notion, as if it
was (as indeed it was by me) *taken for granted*.
Thus far therefore I should hope I may be excused in this Omission ; and as to the Phrase
of *equally following every equal Degree of Sincerity*, Mr. *Pyle* may wrangle about it if he pleases,
but I am confident that there is no Man of
Common Sense, who upon the very first reading
of it would not understand the Meaning of it to
be, that *by how much the more Sincere* a Man is, *by
so much the more he* is in God's Favour. Now
since, as I have shown, by *following* Sincerity,
his Lordship did not *barely* mean that the Favour of God *attended* upon Sincerity, but that
Sincerity gave a Man a *Right* or *Title* to God's
Favour; since likewise, as has been shown, *Sincerity* admits of *no Degrees*, but must be every
where *equally* or *not at all*; the Consequence is
plain, as I have laid it down in my *Remarks*, that
according to his Lordship ALL sincere Persons,
*i. e all those who use their utmost endeavours to in-
form themselves rightly, and act according to the best
of their Judgments*, have a right to an EQUAL
SHARE

SHARE or DEGREE *of the Favour of God.* This,
I fay, is fo clearly the Cafe, that as I *then*
thought that there was no need for me particularly to explain what his Lordfhip meant by
equally following every equal Degree of Sincerity:
So I *now* think I might, without any Prejudice
to his Lordfhip, pafs over all that Mr. *Pyle* has
faid to fhew that I have mifunderftood this Sentence ; which indeed is of fuch a fort, as I never
once faw drop, till now, from the Pen of any
Writer who pretends to be a Man of Senfe and
a Scholar. But becaufe the iffue of the prefent
Controverfy does pretty much depend upon the
Senfe of thefe Words, and becaufe Mr. *Pyle* perhaps would grow angry, and tell me once more,
That much has *been written in Vindication of his
Lordfhip's true and confiftent meaning in thefe Expreffions*———*without the leaft fhadow of a candid
and rational Reply*; I will, I muft, fubmit to the
drudgery of Examining it ; and accordingly I prefent to my *Patient* Reader, the whole Paffage in-
tire, which is as follows.

Had it never at all been fhown, that by equally
following *is naturally to be underftood* proportionably following *the feveral Degrees of* Sincerity,
fo as to reward Sincere Men not all with equal
Happinefs, *but with Happinefs* fuited *and* proportioned *to the feveral Meafures of Virtuous* Qualifications *and* Perfections *Men are endowed with by
the Honeft and* Sincere *ufe of the different Degrees
of Light and Knowledge they have enjoyed* · That
*Sincerity is rewarded as fuch, by its being made the
only, but* fure ground *of Mens being accepted at
all, and becoming proper Subjects of a Reward;
and yet that the feveral Degrees of* Rewards themfelves, *ftill depended upon the different* Advancements *of Men in the ufe of the different Numbers
of Talents committed to them* ; That *in accepting
the*

the Sincerity *of* all *Men without diftinction, as the* Qualification *for a* juft *and* merciful *Reward,* God *acts uniformly, conftantly, and invariably agreeably to the Perfections of his* own *Nature, to the ftricter Relation it has to* our *Nature, and to the Nature of* Things; *but in beftowing on Men feveral different* Degrees of Light, Advantages and Abilities, *and in differently* rewarding '*the different and proportionate* improvements *of thefe,* God does *in the proper Senfe* what he will with his own, *fo that* equal Sincerity *is by him* equally *rewarded, when in it felf confidered, and where nothing* elfe *intervenes to heighten or leffen the Reward : It being confiftently allowed that* greater or lefs Qualifications *going along with equal Degrees of* Sincerity, *may entitle* Perfons equally Sincere, *to different Rewards, in which cafe not the* Sincerity *merely, but the Qualifications render one capable of, and proper for greater Happinefs than another, and yet ftill* equal Sincerity *is* as fuch, or cæteris paribus, *equally refpected* and rewarded · That *this is the moft natural Conftruction of the Bifhop's Expreffions, and fo confiftent with the Tenor of Scripture, and efpecially with the* Famous Parable of the Talents, *and the* 2d *Chapter to the* Romans *compared together, that to imagine my* Lord *could intend any other, were to imagine him void of all common Underftanding, in refpect to either the way of right* Reafoning *or the Senfe of* Scripture . I *fay,* Sir, *had nothing of this been already done———it would have been very pardonable, at leaft much more excufable, for his Adverfaries to have imputed the foregoing Sentiments to him But fince it has been done———for Writers ftill to ftep forth anew, and palm thefe Things afrefh upon us, feems to befpeak a Determination to* Banter, *and not to* Argue. p. 8, 9, 10

So then; we are at laft got to the end of this long-winded Sentence, which contains the whole

D of

of Mr. *Pyle's* Senfe of this Matter ; in which he
has referred to what has afore been faid in *his
own* Book, and in the Writings of *others*, none
of which I have by me but the Bifhop's *Anfwer*
to the *Reprefentation*, and Mr. *Burnet's firft Letter* to Mr. *Law*, in neither of which I can find
any Thing to the Purpofe. But not being willing to miftruft either Mr. *Pyle's* Judgment or
Fidelity, I will fuppofe that he has here given
us a compleat Abftract of all that has been here-
tofore offered upon this Head, and that this
Paffage contains a full Account of what he and
the reft of the Bifhop's Friends fuppofe to be his
Lordfhip's *true confiftent Meaning*, and of their
Reafons for it All this, I fay, for quiets fake
I am willing to fuppofe ; but then there is one
Thing which very much puzzles me ftill, and
that is, to find out the *true confiftent Meaning* of
this Paffage To me, it appears to be a heap of
words without any confiftent Meaning all, fome
giving me up all that I would have, and others
again *taking it away* For inftance. *By* EQUALLY
following, it feems, *is naturally to be underftood*
PROPORTIONABLY *following the feveral Degrees of
Sincerity*—— How Mr *Pyle !* Does *equally* naturally fignify *proportionably ?* I hope not. If I
give to *one* Labourer *two* Shillings for *one* days
Work, and to another *one* Shilling for *half a
days* Work, I reward them both *proportionably*,
but I do not reward them both *equally*. But
that perhaps which Mr.*Pyle* would have faid (and
that which he muft fay, if he has a mind to
fpeak Senfe) is this, That *by equally following*
EVERY EQUAL DEGREE, is naturally to be underftood, or naturally implies *proportionably following the feveral Degrees of Sincerity* ; which is
true, and comes up exactly to what I fay thefe
words imply, *viz* That *by how much the more
Sincere*

Sincere a Man is, *by so much the more* he is *in God's Favour.* But what then does he mean by adding, *So as to reward sincere Men, not all with equal Happiness, but with Happiness suited and proportioned to the several Measures of vertuous Qualifications and Perfections Men are endowed with* BY *the Honest and Sincere use of the different Degrees of Light and Knowledge they have enjoyed?* What I say, does he mean by adding these Words, which contain a Sense as directly opposite to the other as Light is to Darkness? If God proportions his Favour according to the *several Measures* of *Virtuous Qualifications* and *Perfections* which Men have attained unto *by* or *under* Sincerity, as these *last* words imply ; it is not then true what is asserted in the *first, viz.* That he proportions his Favour to the *several Degrees* of *Sincerity* ; Because upon this supposition it may so happen that he who is *less* Sincere may (upon the Account of *greater Improvements*) be *better* Rewarded than he who is *more* Sincere. Mr. *Pyle* confesses as much. *Greater or less Qualifications going along with equal Degrees of Sincerity, may entitle Persons equally Sincere to different Rewards*, and this he says is *consistently allowed.* Consistently! With what, Sir? Certainly not with saying that God proportions his Favour to the *Degrees* of *Sincerity* ; For this necessarily implies, that where the *Sincerity* is *greater*, there the *Reward* will be *greater* ; and where it is *less*, there the *Reward* also will be *less.* In this Case 'tis the Sincerity *merely* that must make the Difference ; whereas in the other, you your self say, That 'tis *not the Sincerity merely, but the Qualifications that render one capable of and proper for greater Happiness than another.* Well; But this you'll say is consistent with affirming that *cæteris paribus* God proportions his Favour to the *several De-*

grees

g.ee. of *Sincerity*, or that equal Sincerity is equally refpected and rewarded *where nothing elfe intervenes to heighten or leffen the Reward* Who doubts it! And is this then at laft what you fay is *the moft natural Conftruction of the Bifhop's Expreffion* ' Why fo it feems indeed But furely, Sir, it is high time for you to have done *Writing*, at leaft, if you can believe *that* to be the *natural Conftruction* of any Sentence, which *alters* the *Nature* of it, and from an *abfolute* Affertion, makes it to become a *limited* one! To fay that *the Favour of God equally follows every equal Degree of Sincerity*, is one Thing. And to fay, That *the Favour of God equally follows every equal Degree of Sincerity* cæteris paribus, *and where nothing elfe intervenes*, &c is another. And therefore if his Lordfhip had had a mind to have been underftood in this latter Senfe, he fhould have added this Claufe ; which fince he has not done, I fee not, for my part, what Right Mr *Pyle* has to *fuppofe* it, unlefs he has a Privilege (which indeed, by his way of Writing, one would think he lays claim to) of making Sentences fignify even juft what he pleafes Mr *Pyle* feems to have been aware of this Objection, and therefore he has taken care to exprefs himfelf in fuch a manner as would induce an unattentive Reader to believe that his Lordfhip *has* indeed added this Claufe His Lordfhip you muft know has made ufe of the Phrafe *os fuch*. Now (fays Mr. *Pyle*) *Equal Sincerity is* as fuch, *or* cæteris paribus *equally refpected and rewarded. As fuch* OR *cæteris paribus!* As if thefe two Phrafes were of the fame Signification ! But every one that has not forgotten his *Accidence*, muft know, that *cæteris paribus* fignifies *when all other Refpects, Circumftances* or *Qualifications are equal.* Now if it be confidered that his Lordfhip has, in the *former part*

part of the Sentence, laid it down as a Principle, that the Favour of God follows Sincerity *confidered as fuch* (*i e* as I have fhown, Sincerity *alone*, or Sincerity *unattended* with any other *Circumſtance* or *Qualification*) and deduced it (N B.) *as a Confequence* from hence, in the latter part, that the Favour of God *equally follows every equal Degree* of Sincerity. If this, I fay, be confidered, it will appear, not only that his Lordfhip has *not added* this Claufe, but that the Sentence really will not *admit* of it. *The Favour of God*, fays his Lordfhip, *follows Sincerity confidered as fuch*, AND CONSEQUENTLY——— *And consequently* What? Why, fays Mr *Pyle*, *and confequently* cæteris paribus *equally follows every equal Degree of Sincerity.* Which is as much as to fay, That BECAUSE the Favour of God follows Sincerity WITHOUT any other *Circumſtance* or *Qualification*, THEREFORE IF, or upon Condition that, all other *Circumſtances* or *Qualifications* BE EQUALL, equal Degrees of Sincerity will be attended with equal Favour How Jejune, how Infipid is this! How (*m*) *mighty an Enchantment muſt this Bifhop of ours, this clear Writer have upon his Pen*, if he can draw up an Argument in which the *Premiſes* and the *Conclufion* bear no *Proportion* or *Relation* the one to the other! Is not this, Mr. *Pyle*, making his Lordfhip *void of all common Underſtanding in refpeɛt to the way of right Reaſoning?* And yet, Sir, this is the very Cafe, if your Interpretation be admitted. For let me ask once more, What does his Lordfhip mean when he fays, that the Favour of God *follows* Sincerity confidered as fuch? Is it that Sincerity is the *only Thing* which God *regards* in

---

(*m*) Ibid. p. 3ɜ.

beſtow-

beftowing his Favour? If fo, then the *Conclufion*
will *contradict* the *Premifes*; for to fay that the
Favour of God equally follows every equal Degree of Sincerity, *then,* and *then only,* when all
other *Circumftances* or *Qualifications* are *equal,* is
to fuppofe that Sincerity is *not* the *only* Thing
that God *regards* in beftowing his Favour. Or
does the Bifhop mean barely this, that Sincerity
is *alone fufficient* to procure, or entitle Men to
God's Favour? This I am fure is the leaft that
can be meant But even then the *Premifes* and
the *Conclufion* will have no *Relation* to one another For the *Premifes* and the *Conclufion* have
then no *Relation* to one another, when the *Truth*
of the *latter* does not at all *depend* upon the *Truth*
of the *former.* Now that all Perfons *equally Sin-*
cere are *cæteris paribus,* or *all other Circumftances*
being equal, equally or *alike* in God's Favour, muft
be acknowledged, if it were only faid, that
Sincerity is *one* among *many* Qualifications which
recommend a Man to God's Favour, and confequently this can have no dependance upon his
Lordfhip's Principle, that Sincerity *alone* is fufficient to procure, or entitle Men to God's Favour.

The fhort of the matter is this; That there
is no way to make his Lordfhip's way of Arguing *juft* and *Logical* (without running extravagantly from the plain and obvious Senfe of the
words) but to fuppofe that his Intention was in
both Parts of the Sentence, to exclude *every*
thing befides *Sincerity* from having *any thing* to do
in *procuring* the Favour of God. Upon this
foot indeed all will be eafy, natural, and ftrong,
as you will quickly perceive by making the Ex-
periment. Try firft, the Argument *forward,*
The Favour of God follows Sincerity *confidered*
as fuch, i e Sincerity is *the only thing* which

God *regards* in beſtowing his Favour. What can be more juſt than from hence to infer, that the Favour of God *equally follows* every *equal Degree* of *Sincerity*, how *differently Qualified* ſoever in *other reſpects* Men may be ? Try it again *backward*; The Favour of God *equally follows* every *equal Degree* of *Sincerity*, i e. all Perſons *equally Sincere* are *equally* or *alike* in God's Favour. What can be more neceſſarily implied under this, than that *Sincerity* is the *only thing* which God *regards* in beſtowing his Favour ? If Mr. *Pyle* could have found out any other expedient by which his Lordſhip's *Premiſes* and his *Concluſion* might be brought to ſo good an Agreement as this, it would have been very much to the purpoſe to have mentioned it. But this of all other Things ſeems to have been the leaſt in his Thoughts. Such was his haſte to make his Lordſhip ſpeak *Truth*, that he never conſider'd how to make him ſpeak *conſiſtently*, or whether the Senſe which he had put upon his words were agreeable to that *Relation* which the ſeveral Parts of the Sentence bear to one another; for which *judicious* management, how much he deſerves his Lordſhip's Thanks, I ſhall leave them to agree among themſelves—— But what need is there for me to perſue this Point any faither, when his Lordſhip's *laſt Words* conſidered *by themſelves* and *without* any manner of *regard had* to what *goes before*, are *alone* ſufficient to bear me out ? I do inſiſt upon it, and for ever ſhall inſiſt upon it in oppoſition to his Lordſhip and all his Friends, that to ſay that The Favour of God *equally follows every equal Degree of Sincerity*, can imply no leſs than that *by how much* the more *Sincere* a Man is, *by ſo much the more* he is in *God's Favour*. That therefore this Sentence *of it ſelf*, and without any thing elſe *conſidered with*, or added

ded

ded to it, does effectually and necessarily exclude *every thing* but Sincerity, from having *any thing to do* in procuring God's Favour And that Mr. *Pyle*, by adding the Clause *cæteris paribus*, (which his Lordship himself never added) has taken an unjustifiable Liberty ; such a Liberty as if it were admitted in all like Cases, no Words or Sentences could have any fixed and determinate meaning, but must depend entirely upon the Arbitrary Will and Pleasure of him who undertakes to interpret them. Suppose that I should any where have affirmed that *all* who acknowledge King *George*'s Title, and have taken the *Oaths* of *Allegiance*, &c are *equally* Friends to his Administration ; No doubt but his Lordship and those of his Party would accuse me as having asserted a notorious Falsehood But I will maintain *this* and almost any thing else, if I may be allowed the same Liberty that Mr. *Pyle* has allowed himself For when such a Sentence comes to be examined, and I find my self at a loss how to defend it, 'tis but clapping in a *cæteris paribus*, and the business is done. Since how false soever the Assertion may be *without* that Clause, *with it* it must be certainly and undeniably true Instances of this sort need not be multiplied Every one sees that there can be no such Thing as disputing upon the Sense of a Passage in any Author, if those who engage in the Debate may take upon themselves to put in words which give that Passage a Sense quite different from, and even contrary to, what, as it stands, it does naturally import. But tho' I thus complain of Mr. *Pyle* in point of *justice*, yet I cannot but commend him in point of *Policy*. For since, as I very plainly perceive, he is fully resolved that his Lordship SHALL be always in the *right*, and all his Opponents for ever in the

wrong

wrong; 'twas certainly his wifeſt way to endea-vour, with all ſpeed, to reconcile the World to this and ſome other ſuch like Artifices, which he has found it neceſſary, for the carrying of his Point, to have recourſe to more than once, as will be ſeen in the ſubſequent Parts of this Diſcourſe

Upon the whole then I conclude ; That his Lordſhip's Poſition, according to the *Natural* and *Grammatical* Conſtruction of it, implies what in my *Remarks* I have ſuppoſed it to imply, *viz.* That the Sincerity of a Man's Heart is the *only* Thing which God *regards* in diſpenſing his Favour. And let not Mr *Pyle* take it ill to be told that, whether he knows it or not, he has aſſerted the ſame thing expreſly in this very Paſ-ſage upon which I am now remarking *Sincerity,* ſays he, *is the* ONLY GROUND *of Mens being ac-cepted at all, and becoming proper Subjects of a Re-ward,* i e Sincerity is the *only Reaſon* or *Mo-tive* upon which God *accepts* and *rewards* any Man, or, which is the ſame thing, Sincerity is the *only Thing* which in that Caſe God has any *regard* to. Now whereas he adds, that *yet,* or notwithſtanding this, *the ſeveral Degrees of Rewards themſelves depend upon the different Ad-vancements of Men in the uſe of the different Num-bers of Talents committed to them* ; in this he has only farther manifeſted his own inconſiſtency. For theſe *Advancements,* whatever they be, are certainly ſomething *diſtinct* from Sincerity. Now if *nothing but* Sincerity, or (which is all one) nothing *diſtinct from* Sincerity, is a *Reaſon* or *Motive* with God to *accept* or *reward* any Man, then the *ſeveral Degrees* of *Rewards* can depend upon *nothing but* Sincerity. For certainly that which is not a *Reaſon* or *Motive* with God why a Man ſhould be *at all* rewarded, can never

E   be

be a *Reason* or *Motive* with him why he should be *better* rewarded.

When Mr *Pyle* will be pleased to write so clearly upon this Point, as that we may certainly know what he would deny and what he would affirm, we shall have more Encouragement to Debate it farther with him. In the mean while, since by all that can be gathered from what he has said, it appears that he is not able to put any other found and consistent Sense upon the Bishop's Words than what I have already put upon them, I shall look upon my self to be thus far justified, and proceed to the other Parts of his Book Indeed I am almost ashamed that I have spent so many words upon a matter, upon which (had it not been for humouring Mr *Pyle*) none at all would have been necessary. But when Men are set upon wrangling, it is good sometimes to follow them in their own way; and if by what I have now offered this Gentleman should be brought to consider the Case with a little more Temper and Judgment, I shall not think my time ill bestowed; though, to say the Truth, 'tis what I do not mightily expect from him.

C H A P.

CHAP. III.

Containing an Answer to Mr. Pyle's *Exceptions against the* Consequences *drawn from his Lordship's* Position.

HAving thus secured the *Foundation* of my *Remarks*, by shewing that I have not mistaken the Sense of his Lordship's words, we shall be the better able to maintain the *Superstructure* which is built upon it ; which consists of several *Consequences* drawn before by the Learned *Committee*, and by me reduced to this *general one*, viz. That *all sincere Persons*, or (for it is the same Thing) all Persons *equally Sincere, have equally a Right or Title to God's Favour*, i. e. (for this I confess was my meaning) have a Right to an *equal Share* or *Measure* of God's Favour, *whatsoever Method of Religion they follow*. If the Reader will turn to *page* 3 of my *Remarks*, he will find those *Consequences* set down, together with the *Reasons* by which they are supported : I think it no more needful to repeat them here, than I do to take Notice of those *Eighteen* or *Twenty Lines* which Mr *Pyle* has (*n*) written about them, which I must be contented to let rest under those Clouds of obscurity, which this Author delights perpetually to wrap himself up in, when he wants something to say. Every common Reader will understand that those *Consequences* must needs follow from his Lordship's *Position*, if that *general Inference* just now mentioned, in which, according to Mr.

(*n*) Ibid. *p.* 10.

Pyle's

Pyle's own Confeſſion, I have (*o*) *rightly ſumm'd
them all up*, does follow from it And that it
does follow from it, I cannot miſtruſt either
Mr. *Pyle*'s Senſe or Modeſty ſo much as to think
he will now deny. For indeed, that *all ſincere
Perſons have a right to an equal Share or Degree of
God's Favour* (which I have ſhewn to be what
his Lordſhip's *Poſition* imports) and that *all ſincere Perſons have a Right to an equal Share or Degree of God's Favour, whatever Method of Religion they follow* (which is the general *Inference*
drawn by me from that Poſition) are Sentences
between which there is no other Difference than
this, *viz.* That the *latter* is *leſs general* than,
and conſequently muſt needs be *included* under
the *former*.

But this it ſeems is an (*p*) *Abſurdity, never ſo
much as thought of by his Lordſhip or any of his Advocates* And what is that to me ? If his Lordſhip and his Advocates cannot underſtand the
true and neceſſary Conſequences of their own
Doctrines; or if they expreſs themſelves in
words which carry a different Senſe from what
they really intend, let them look to it. I have
nothing to do with Mens *Thoughts* any farther
than they appear from their *Words*, and according to this Rule of judging, I will venture to
ſay, that *I* know of *one* of his Lordſhip's *Advocates* who *thought of* this *Abſurdity*, and that is
Mr. *Pyle himſelf*, who has aſſerted it in as plain
Terms as poſſible Out of many Paſſages which
might be produced to prove this, I ſhall content my ſelf to ſelect One, which I find drag'd
in where it has nothing to do ; pertinent Matter having, as I ſuppoſe, been very ſcarce, or

---

(*o*) Ibid. (*p*) Ibid.

in hopes, it may be, that standing thus out of
the way, it might not be so readily taken Notice of on this Occasion. But it is by much too
material to be overlooked, and therefore Reader take it entire as follows.

The only Question is, What that Respect *or Relation was in which his Lordship is charged to have*
put all Communions upon the level, *as to sincere*
Men '*Tis agreed upon to be the* Favour of God,
the Justification of all such Men before God, *or*
the Salvation of Men. *And here, Sir, comes in*
the Foundation of all this Misunderstanding ; 'Tis
here Mr. Stebbing *may please to see the Original of*
his Own, and of the Committee's *Misrepresentati-*
on. His Lordship, most evidently, by God's Favour, Justification, *and* Salvation, *means* one
Thing, while they *are determined to mean* another.
Take it in the Bishop's Sense, for that general Favour of God *toward* Sincerity, *which terminates*
uniformly in saving all Sincere Persons from Con-
demnation, *and bestowing on them Rewards* proportionate *to their several* Qualifications *and* Advancements *in* Real Religion ; *and then 'tis cer-*
tainly clear, that the Intrinsick Goodness *of one*
Method *above another, does not at all come into*
Consideration; all being thus far justified by vertue
of the mere Sincerity *of their* Choices *But take*
it in their Sense, for that Favour *and* Justification
which terminates in equal Rewards *to be given to*
all Sincere Persons, Christian, Jewish, *and* Hea-
thenish *alike ; and then 'twere an Absurdity indeed*
to affirm intrinsick Goodness *to make no Diffe-*
rence, when 'tis that alone that qualifies one Man
for being a Subject proper and fit for greater future
Glories *than another,* p. 13.

I have recited this Passage at large, because I
would leave Mr. *Pyle* no room to say that I
have wrong'd him ; and now before I make that
use

ufe of it which I principally intend, I will beg
of the Reader to take notice how abfurdly he
has crowded the very *Point* in Debate, into
that which he pretends is only an *Explication* of
the *Terms* of the Queftion. By the *Favour* of
God and *Juftification*, fays he, the Bifhop means
THAT *Favour* of God towards Sincerity *which
terminates in proportionate Rewards*, whereas the
Committee mean THAT *Favour which terminates
in equal Rewards.* That Favour which terminates——! What Stuff is this! Why the very
Queftion, Sir, is *where* the *Favour* of God *terminates*; *i e* whether it *terminates in equal Rewards*
upon upon *all* fincere Perfons *whatever Method
of Religion they follow!* Now if your meaning be
to fay, that by the *Favour of God* the Bifhop
means *that Favour* which does NOT *terminate
in equal Rewards* upon *all* fincere Perfons *whatfoever Method of Religion they have followed* (which
muft be the cafe if you mean to fay any thing
to the Purpofe) who fees not that under the
Notion of *explaining Terms*, you directly *beg* the
thing that is to be *proved?* To fay what is
meant by the *Favour of God*, is one thing, and
to fay *where* the *Favour* of God *terminates*, is
another. And therefore, Sir, for you under
the pretence of doing the *former*, to tell us any
thing relating to the *latter*, is juft as pertinent
as it would be if whilft you are giving a general Defcription of a *Houfe*, you fhould take upon
you to fay, how *long* or how *wide* it is—— But
this by the way That which I produce this
Paffage for, is to fhew, that Mr. *Pyle* (by a *fata-
lity* not unufual to him) has in this very Paffage
owned that to be *the Bifhop's Senfe*, which yet he,
in the *fame Paffage*, labours to prove is falfly
charged upon him by the *Committee*, and my felf.
For pray obferve; He declares it to be his

Lord-

Lordſhip's Sence, *That the Favour of God terminates in ſaving all ſincere Perſons from Condemna-
tion, and beſtowing upon them Rewards proportionate to their ſeveral Qualifications and Advancements in real Religion.* By the *Advancements* of
Men *in real Religion,* you are to underſtand thoſe
*virtuous Perfections which they are endowed with
by the honeſt and ſincere uſe of that Light or Knowledge they have enjoyed* Theſe, together with *Sincerity* in the *Choice* of thoſe *particular Methods*
of *Religion* which Men have followed, were, as
you may remember, *afore* declared to be the
Rule or *Meaſure* according to which God proceeds in *proportionating* the *ſeveral Degrees* of
Favour and *Happineſs* in a Life to come. Here
again they are declared to be the *Rule* and the
only Rule, in oppoſition to the *Method* of *Religion*
which is *expreſly* excluded from having any thing
to do in the Matter. For if it be asked whether
God, in *proportionating* his *Favours* or *Rewards*
hereafter, will not regard *the Goodneſs* of thoſe
Methods of *Religion* which Men have followed,
as well as their *Advancements* in *Real Religion*;
Mr. *Pyle* anſwers in his own and in the Biſhop's
Name, *It is certainly clear that the* INTRINSICK
GOODNESS *of one Method above another does not
at all come into Conſideration* All, ſays he,
are *thus far juſtified by Vertue of the mere Sincerity
of their Choices.* That is to ſay, If a Man be
but *Sincere* in his *Choice* of that *Method of Religion* which he follows, *he* and *all ſuch* ſhall be *ſo
far* juſtified, that whether the *Methods* they have
followed be *good,* or whether they be *bad,* yet
they ſhall every one of them be Rewarded in a
Meaſure proportionate to thoſe *Degrees* of *Virtuous*
or *Moral Perfections,* which they have each of
them ſeverally attained unto. So that if we
put the Caſe of *two* Perſons equally advanced in
Moral

Moral Honefty; the *one* a *Chriftian*, and the other *no Chriftian* : The *Chriftian* will have nothing to plead from his *being a Chriftian*; God will not confider, that the *one* by having *believed* in his *Son*, and having been *Baptized* in his *Name*, has been taken into a *Special Covenant* with himfelf, which the *other* has not; he will not confider that the *one* hath purfued *that Method* of *Religion* which he hath *prefcribed*, and whereof he *approves*, and that the *other* hath followed *another Method* which he hath *not prefcribed*, and whereof he doth *not approve*; all this I fay will be no Motive with God to Reward *the one better* than he rewards *the other*; no, they are both intitled to an *equal* Reward *merely* in vertue of their *Sincerity*, and becaufe they are *equal Proficients* in *Moral Qualifications*.

This is fo clearly the Senfe and Tendency of what Mr *Pyle* has afferted in this Paffage, that I fhall venture to tell him before-hand, that if hereafter he fhall perfift in affirming that *it was never in his Thoughts* to fay, That *all fincere Perfons have equally a Right and Title to God's Favour*, i e *to equal Degrees of future Happinefs or Reward, whatfoever Method of Religion they follow*; he will hereby very plainly fhew, either that he does not underftand the meaning of what he fays himfelf, or elfe that he knows not the very Senfe of that Queftion about which we are now difputing. The Queftion in fhort is this : Whether the *Method* of *Religion* which a Man follows *confidered as fuch*, or *confidered as it is a Method of Religion* of this or of that fort, will make *any difference* as to a Man's *Salvation* or *future Happinefs* And if Mr *Pyle* has not here affirmed it as his own and the Bifhop's Senfe, that *it makes no difference*, it will be impoffible that it ever fhould be affirmed, feeing it is impoffible that any words can be found out by which it can be

more

more clearly and more fully expressed. Nor let it be objected that this Author declares a little after, that it is an *Absurdity to affirm, that the intrinsick Goodness* of one Method of Religion above a nother *makes no difference* ; For tho' *this*, as these words do really signify, and as they ought to be underftood, is indeed a flat contradiction ; yet according as Mr. *Pyle* undeistands thefe words, or in the fenfe wherein *he* fpeaks them, they are very reconcileable with that which I now fay is his Opinion in the Cafe What Mr *Pyle* means when he fays, that the *intrinfick Goodnefs* of one *Method* above another *does* make a difference, we may gather from the *Reafon* he has given *why* it makes a Difference, which is this, that it is the *intrinfick Goodnefs* of one Method above another *alone, that qualifies one Man for being a Subject proper and fit for greater future Glories than another.* Qualifies ? How ? Why not *confidered merely as it is a Method of Religion intrinfically better* than another For Mr *Pyle*, to be fure, would not fay, nor indeed do we pretend, that this *Confideration* is that *alone*, or the *only* thing which qualifies for greater Glories The Senfe therefore muft be this, that the *intrinfick Goodnefs* of one *Method* of Religion above another makes a Difference, becaufe it is this alone that leads *to greater moral Perfections*, and *fo* qualifies a Man for being a Subject proper and fit for greater Glories Now if this be all, it will ftill be true that the intrinfick Goodnefs *as fuch* makes *no Difference* For if *one* Method of Religion does *therefore only* qualify for greater Glories than *another, becaufe* it leads to greater *moral Perfections* ; 'tis plain that the reafon why *one* Man is *better rewarded* than *another*, muft ftill only be, becaufe he has *greater* moral Perfections than another ;

F   which

which is to say, that 'tis *not* the *intrinfick Good-nefs* of the Method *as fuch*, but the *different improvements* and *advancements* under that Method, which makes *the Difference*

Thus then it appears, that according to the account which M^{Pyle} himfelf has given us of the matter, there would be no wrong done to the Bifhop, if we fhould fay that his *Defign* was to teach, that all fincere Perfons are entitled to an equal Share or Degree of God's Favour, whatever Method of Religion they follow And indeed I can fee no manner of Reafon to doubt it, whether Mr *Pyle* will acknowledge it or not. Every one knows that the Difcourfe about the availablenefs of *Sincerity* to the Juftification of *all Perfons* under *different Communions,* was that which gave occafion to that Pofition of his Lordfhip, upon which I have made my Remarks ; and how is it poffible to fuppofe that his Loidfhip fhould *not intend* to *include* under his *general Rule* that *particular Cafe* by which his *general Rule* was *introduced ?* Befides, the Bifhop himfelf exprefly tells us, (*Preferv* p 90) that a Man's *Title to God's Favour cannot depend upon his actual being or continuing in any particular Method of Religion, but upon his real Sincerity,* &c And what I pray is this, but to fay, that if a Man be but fincere, whatever Method of Religion he follows, his Title to God's Favour will be the fame ? For if it be faid either that fome Methods of Religion will not *at all* entitle a Man to God's Favour, or even that *one* Method will entitle a Man to a greater fhare of God's Favour than *another*, it will be ridiculous to fay that a Man's Title to God's Favour does *not* depend upon his following any particular Method, *but* upon Sincerity, becaufe upon either of thefe Suppofitions it muft in fome fort at leaft depend upon *both*.———But, as I have
often

often faid, *not* his Lordſhip's *Intentions*, but the *true Conſequences* of his *Doctrines* are the proper Subject of my Enquiry: And therefore if his general Principle, according to the plain and obvious Conſtruction of it, does imply that all ſincere Perſons have a Title to an equal Share or Degree of God's Favour, whatever Method of Religion they follow, I have nothing more to do in the matter.

Having in my *Remarks* juſtified the *Conſequences* of his Lordſhip's Doctrine as ſtated by the *Committee*, my next Buſineſs was to conſider his Lordſhip's *Exceptions* againſt theſe *Conſequences*, and in doing this I have very plainly ſhewn in *one* inſtance, that his Lordſhip hath very greatly miſtaken the Senſe of the *Committee*, and in the *reſt* that he hath artfully avoided ſaying that, which, would he have ſpoken his mind plainly out, he would have found himſelf under a neceſſity of acknowledging. Againſt this part of my Book Mr. *Pyle* has written very particularly, but in ſuch a manner, that 'tis with reluctancy I enter upon the examination of it; in which I muſt be obliged to lay open ſuch Inſtances of—— the Reader will ſee what, as I am ſorry and aſhamed ſhould ever be found in a *Chriſtian* and a *Clergyman*. But foraſmuch as this is neceſſary towards my own Defence, who am on the other hand treated as one who has uſed his Lordſhip very unfairly; and becauſe it is proper upon another account, that the World ſhould be throughly convinced with what ſort of *Spirit* this Author writes; I ſhall therefore ſubmit to the ungrateful Task; and if herein I ſhall ſay ſome things (tho' I will take care to ſay as few as I can) which are not ſo much for Mr. *Pyle*'s Advantage, as he himſelf muſt needs be ſenſible; ſo I hope thoſe about us will do me the juſtice to conſider,

who

who 'tis that gave the occasion for it. To be-
gin then.

The *first* Consequence mentioned by me as
charged upon his Lordship's Doctrine by the
Committee, is, that it makes *all Methods of Religion alike, and puts all Communions upon an equal
Foot*, &c His Lordship's Answer to this Charge
was set down in his own words, to wit; That
*what he had said about private Perswasion related to
the Justification of the Man before God, and not to
the excellency of one Communion above another, which
it leaves just as it finds it, and cannot possibly alter.*
Hereupon I observed it as a very manifest Case,
that his Lordship *supposed* the meaning of the
Committee to be, that he had made all Methods
of Religion alike, and put all Communions upon
an equal foot, WITH RESPECT TO *to their real natural and intrinsick Excellency*; whereas indeed
the Case was quite otherwise; for that the *Committee* had only said that his Lordship had put all
Communions upon an equal Foot, WITHOUT RE-
GARD TO *any intrinsick Goodness*; and had declared
in express words, that he had made all Methods
alike (not *in respect* to their *intrinsick Goodness,*
but) *in respect* TO SALVATION or the FAVOUR of
GOD. This is the substance of my Answer, which
the Reader may there find pursued at large, and
justified in every particular And what now says
Mr. *Pyle* to this? Why in the first place, and
without any Ceremony he charges me with the
worst sort of *Imposture* a Writer can be guilty of!
(*r*) *How,* says he, *are they* (the Committee)
*brought off from this Misrepresentation? Why by
turning upon his Lordship a false Quotation* ———
This, Mr *Pyle,* is a very heavy Charge, and ac-

(r) Ibid p 12.

cording as it appears to be either true or falſe, it will appear that either you or I are the moſt a-bandon'd of Men 'Tis not fit that the Matter ſhould remain long in ſuſpenſe, and to my great Comfort I believe that there is not a Reader up-on the Earth, either ſo very careleſs, or ſo void of Underſtanding, as not inſtantly to ſee on whoſe Shoulders the Burden will fall. It ſeems this *falſe Quotation* which I have *trumped* upon his Lordſhip, is a falſe Quotation *of the Commit-tee's words,* i e I have made the Biſhop to have quoted the *Committee* falſely If ſo, then I muſt have quoted the Biſhop falſly. But how is this? Why thus; I have *made him ſay* WITH RESPECT TO, *inſtead of* WITHOUT REGARD TO, i e. I have made the Biſhop *cite the Committee as ſaying* (for this is what Mr. *Pyle* means) *with reſpect to,* inſtead of *without regard to* Now, ſays Mr *Pyle, I can find no ſuch change made by the Biſhop in the* 113 *page of his Lordſhip's Anſwer referred to by M.* Stebbing. *The word is as it ſtands in the* Committee's *Repre-ſentation,* WITHOUT, *and there is no alteration of it into* WITH This, Reader, is the whole of the Caſe, by which you perceive that this Charge of Mr. *Pyle* is every whit as *Weak* as it is *Malicious.* For the truth is, that I never once quoted the Biſhop as having *altered the Words* of the Com-mittee, but only as having *miſtaken the meaning* of thoſe Words. I do indeed ſay, that *what his Lordſhip* REPRESENTS *the Committee as ſaying, is, that he hath put all Communions upon an equal Foot* WITH RESPECT TO *their intrinſick Goodneſs* But *how* has he *repreſented* the *Committee* as ſaying this? Why plainly, not by *altering the Words* of the *Repreſentation,* but by what he ſays *in Anſwer* to them, the Scope and Tenor of which is ſuch as evidently ſhews that he *underſtood* the Charge of the *Committee* to be, that he had *put all Communi-*

ons

ons upon an equal Foot WITH RESPECT TO *their in-trinfick Goodnefs*. If Mr *Pyle* will fay that the Bishop did *not* underftand the Charge of the *Committee* in this Senfe, he will make him to prevaricate moft egregioufly, it being manifeft that the whole of what his Lordship hath offered in direct Anfwer to that Charge, tends only to shew that a Man's *private Perfwafion* doth not *alter* the *effential Nature*, or *intrinfick Worth* of any Communion. Witnefs what he hath faid in the Paffage juft now mentioned, and by me fet down in my *Remarks*; witnefs again the famous Inftance of *Parliamentary Debates* applied by the Bishop himfelf, and taken notice of by Mr *Pyle*, as applicable to this Cafe, in which Inftance his Lordship fays, That *a Man's giving his Vote according to his Perfwafion does not* AFFECT *the* NATURE *of things*; but that notwithftanding this *the fame difference ftill remains between the two fides of any Queftion; and the fame Excellency of one above another*. All this is nothing to the purpofe, if the *Committee* did not charge him with *deftroying* the *intrinfick Worth* and *Excellency* of one Communion above another, or (which is all one) of putting all Communions upon an equal Foot, *with refpect to their intrinfick Worth* and *Excellency*; and if his Lordship did not *underftand* the Charge of the *Committee* in this Senfe, I fay that he has *prevaricated* as well as argued impertinently. But the Charge of the *Committee* is, that he hath put all Communions upon an equal Foot, *without regard to any intrinfick Goodnefs*, and confequently his Lordship muft have miftaken the meaning of this Charge, unlefs to put all Communions upon an equal Foot *without regard to* any *intrinfick Goodnefs*, and to put all Communions upon an equal Foot *with refpect to* their intrinfick Goodnefs, be one and the fame thing. Do then thefe

two

two different Expreffions fignify the fame thing, or do they not? Why yes! Mr *Pyle* has the Hardinefs to maintain that they do! For having given over his *Trumping* (Confcious, without doubt, that it would never carry him through) he prefently lays in for an *After-game*; and as if it were on purpofe to let us know that he was refolved to ftick at nothing, fays, *And yet at laft in which foever of the two ways you exprefs it, I can for my part fee no poffible difference in the Senfe as to the prefent Argument. For* ——now comes the Reafon, fuch a one as it is, *he that is faid to put all Communions upon the Level,* WITHOUT REGARD TO *any intrinfick Goodnefs, may mean no more than this; that intrinfick Goodnefs does not at all come into the confideration of that Relation, wherein 'tis affirmed they are equal; and can mean no lefs than that 'twere the fame thing as to fuch Relation, whether there were any intrinfick Goodnefs of one above the other. And he that is faid to put all Communions upon an equal Foot,* WITH RESPECT TO *intrinfick Goodnefs, cannot be faid to mean any otherwife than that intrinfick Goodnefs can make no difference as to* THAT, *wherein he affirms they are upon an equal Foot, which* my Logick *tells me, are one and the fame thing* ——Now Mr *Pyle* is crept into the dark, and thinks himfelf as fafe as may be. But alas! the Truth is vifible amidft all this Obfcurity; even *Reams* of *Nonfenfe* will not be able to deface it. The *difference* manifeftly is as I have ftated it in my *Remarks*, viz That whereas to fay, that all Communions are upon an equal Foot, *with refpect to* their *intrinfick Goodnefs*, is to fay that the *intrinfick Goodnefs* of all Communions is *the fame,* or that there is *no difference* between the *intrinfick Goodnefs* of *one* Communion, and the *intrinfick Goodnefs* of *another*, to fay that

all

all Communions are put upon an equal Foot, *without regard to* any *intrinfick Goodnefs,* on the contrary fuppofes that there *is a difference* between *the intrinfick Goodnefs* of *one* Communion, and the *intrinfick Goodnefs* of *another,* and is only to affirm that *with refpect* to *fome thing elfe* (which in the prefent Cafe is *Salvation* or *the Favour of God*) all Communions are put upon an equal Foot, *without regarding* or *confidering* that Difference. This is the Truth of the Cafe; and if Mr *Pyle* cannot fee it, it will be the Bufinefs of his *Phyfician* to try to help him, and not mine. But it is plain that he himfelf cannot make any thing elfe of it. For, pray attend a little; He fays in the Paffage juft now fet down, that to affirm that *all Communions are put upon an equal Foot,* or *upon the Level,* WITHOUT REGARD TO ANY *intrinfick Goodnefs, means neither more nor lefs than this,* viz. That it is made to be *the fame thing as to that Refpect or Relation, wherein 'tis affirmed that they are Equal,* or upon the Level, *whether there were any intrinfick Goodnefs of one above another or no.* Now fince that *Refpect* or *Relation* in which his Lordfhip is charged by the *Committee,* to have *put all Communions upon an equal Foot,* is as I have fhewn, and as Mr *Pyle* himfelf grants in the very next Page, *Salvation,* and *the Favour of God;* *'tis evident then that according* to Mr *Pyle's* own Account, the meaning of the Charge of the *Committee* is neither more nor lefs than this, *viz.* That according to his Lordfhip *it is the fame thing as to Salvation, and the Favour of God, whether there were any intrinfick Goodnefs of one Communion above another or no* ; which is the very thing that I fay was meant by the *Committee.* Well then ; is there no difference between faying this, and faying that *all Communions are upon an equal Foot* WITH RESPECT TO *their intrinfick Goodnefs* ?
Why

Why no; Mr. *Pyle*'s Logick *tells* him *that they are one and the same thing* For it seems he who says this *cannot mean any otherwise than that intrinsick Goodness, can make no difference as to* THAT, *wherein he affirms they are upon an equal Foot.* Cannot mean any otherwise! But I say, Sir, that if he means to speak Sense, he cannot *but* mean otherwise; for the *Intrinsick Goodness* is now *it self* that very *Respect* or *Relation* in which all Communions are affirmed to be *upon an equal Foot,* and consequently the *Intrinsick Goodness* cannot be said to make no difference *as to that in which they are affirmed to be upon an equal Foot.* For this were to say that *the Intrinsick Goodness of any Communion can make no Difference as to the Intrinsick Goodness of any Communion,* which how agreeable, Sir, soever it may be to your *Logick,* I am sure is not agreeable to *common Sense* ——— But I shall dispute no longer upon the Difference of these two Expressions, which indeed is so plain of it self, that it is not possible by any thing that can be said to make it plainer We may even grant to Mr. *Pyle* that they are *the same,* and with pleasure observe, how unfortunately he has changed Sides, and left the Bishop and himself in the Lurch. The *Committee* had charged his Lordship with putting all Communions upon an equal Foot, *without Regard to* any Intrinsick Goodness Now *this much* is certain, that his Lordship understood, and all along argued against this as a Charge that he had *destroyed* all *Intrinsick Excellency* between *one Communion* and *another.* If you doubt of this, you may have Mr *Pyle*'s own Word for it. (s) *One cannot,* says he, *be accused of Partiality, in imagining their*

_____

(s) Ibid. p. 14.

the

(the Committee's) *real Intention was to accuse my
Lord of destroying all Internal Excellency, or Truth
of one Religion above another, in the foregoing
Charge, of putting all Religion upon an equal Foot.*
Be not too pofitive, Sir, you'll be convicted of
Partiality, and fomething elfe, before you are
aware of it. For let me ask you ; Does the
Charge of the *Committee imply* that the Bifhop had
deftroyed all *Internal Excellency,* or *Truth* of one
Religion or Communion *above another ?* No, you
your felf fay (as I have fhown juft now) that the
meaning of the Charge of the Committee is neither more nor lefs than this, *viz.* That according to his Lordfhip, *it is the fame thing as to
Salvation and the Favour of God,* WHETHER THERE
WERE any *Intrinfick Goodnefs* of one Communion
above another, and you fay right ; for to fay
that all Communions are put upon an equal
Foot, *without Regard to* any Intrinfick Goodnefs,
efpecially if you add, *or whether they be right or
wrong* (which are the Words of the *Reprefentation*) is fo far from implying that all Intrinfick
Goodnefs is *deftroyed,* that it implies the *direct
contrary,* as has already been obferved. But it
feems if the *Committee* had faid that the Bifhop
had put all Communions upon an equal Foot,
with Refpect to their Intrinfick Goodnefs, even
this would not have done the Bufinefs ; for there
is no difference you fay between thefe two Expreffions, and you tell us exprefly, that (*t*) NEI-
THER *of them conclude any abfolute* DESTRUCTION
*of the Intrinfick Goodnefs of one Communion above
another, as I think one of them does.* I do ftill
think, Sir, that *one* of them does ; but that is
not now the Point between us. *You fay that nei-*

ther of them does, and therefore in *your* Account That ufed by the *Committee*, which is *one* of them, does *not*. But for God's fake, Sir, how can you clear either the Bifhop or your felf from Injuftice and Impertinence in laying it at the *Committee's* Door, that they have charged him with DESTROYING *all Internal Excellency*, or *Truth of one Communion above another*, when as your felf fay their Words imply *no fuch thing* ! ——Here, Sir, I leave you to anfwer for your felf; and your Anfwer is this, *That* IF EITHER *of thefe Expreffions conclude an abfolute* DESTRUCTION *of the Intrinfick Goodnefs of one Communion above another, that of the* Committee *bids the faireft for it of the two* ; WITHOUT REGARD TO *any Intrinfick Goodnefs,* LOOKING MUCH MORE LIKE *a denying all Intrinfick Goodnefs, than the other manner of expreffing it does.* Which if it does not more than *look like* a Determination in you to ftick faft to your Caufe, either *with* or *againft* Reafon, I fhall be content to leave to every impartial Reader to confider.

Mr. *Pyle* having managed this Point fo unfuccefsfully, as you have now feen, a *Silent* Retreat might have well become him. However hef ets a good Face on the Matter, and crys out with the Air of a Conqueror, *Enough in all Reafon upon a poor Quibble.* After this he undertakes to (*u*) *deal with another Quibble,* which, *if it be poffible,* he fays, *is inferior to the former* Now the Matter in fhort is this; That whereas the *Committee* had objected againft his Lordfhip, that *in following any particular Communion he had referred every Man to his own* PRIVATE JUDGMENT, *as that which will juftify even the* WORST *Choice he can*

(*u*) Ibid. p. 14.

G 2 *make* ;

make; and whereas his Lordſhip had alledged
that, CONTRARY *to this Repreſentation, he had never taught that the Sincerity of a Man's private
Judgment will juſtify him in any but the BEST
Choice he can make* My Anſwer is, That herein
his Lordſhip hath not denyed any thing which
the *Committee* hath affirmed; that in the Senſe of
the *Committee* that may be the WORST *Choice,*
which in the Senſe of his Lordſhip is ſtill the
BEST *Choice;* and conſequently that his Lordſhip, inſtead of *removing* this Charge, has only
evaded it I am not in the leaſt diſpleaſed to hear
Mr *Pyle* calling this Anſwer a *Quibble;* for I am
by this time ſo well uſed to him, that wherever
I find this Word, *there* I conclude that I ſhall
certainly meet with ſomething or other which
he knows not how to deal with Whether this
be not the Caſe here, will appear upon Tryal.
Mr *Pyle,* after his uſual way, has ſaid a great
deal upon this Head which might very well
have been ſpared; but every one ſees that the
whole Strength of the Debate muſt lye in thoſe
Paſſages, where he has gone about to explain
what the *Committee* may be ſuppoſed to have
meant by *juſtifying a Man in the* WORST CHOICE
he can make (for concerning the Biſhop's Senſe of
juſtifying in the BEST CHOICE, we have no difference) and conſequently that theſe Paſſages contain the whole of what is neceſſary to be conſidered. Hear him then *What can be the obvious
intended meaning of theſe Words,* JUSTIFY THE
WORST CHOICE, *but either juſtifying or making it
equally Intrinſically Good, with that which is Intrinſically, or in it ſelf the beſt Choice,* i. e *making
that to be in it ſelf true, which is in it ſelf falſe; or
elſe that it will juſtify him in* ANY *Choice, how* BADLY,
INCONSIDERAITLY *and* RASHLY *ſoever made?* This

I

I ſay, as 'tis worded by the Committee, *does ſo naturally carry one of theſe Senſes that*——Yes, Mr. *Pyle* ; *ſo naturally*, that it cannot poſſibly carry *either of them*, unleſs it be to *your ſelf*, who can ſee any Senſe in Words that you have a mind to When the *Committee* ſay that a Man's Private Judgment will *juſtify*, they mean (what only they can in ſound Senſe be ſuppoſed to mean) that it will *juſtify* THE MAN, *i. e.* it will juſtify him *before God*. And thus his Lordſhip himſelf underſtood them. *I am charged* (ſays he, in his *Anſwer* to the *Repreſentation*) *with maintaining that the* MAN's *Private Judgment will juſtify* HIM IN *the worſt Choice he can make,* i e *it will juſtify the Man*, although the Choice which he makes be *the worſt*. So that the word *Juſtify* relating not to the *Choice*, but to *the Man* who makes that Choice ; 'tis ridiculous in you to pretend that the meaning of the *Committee* might be to ſay, that his Lordſhip had made the *worſt Choice* equally Intrinſically Good, with that which is Intrinſically *the beſt Choice*, which indeed is a very manifeſt Contradiction. But may not the meaning of theſe Words be, that a Man's Private Judgment will juſtify him in *any* Choice, however *badly, inconſiderately*, and *raſhly* made? Mr. *Pyle* thinks it may, and this in effect is what the Biſhop has ſuppoſed to be the Senſe of the *Committee* : But I may venture to leave it to any impartial Man to conſider, whether it be poſſible to ſuppoſe that the *Committee* intended any ſuch Charge as this, when it is ſo notoriouſly evident that the words themſelves will not allow of it I ſay it again (for I can ſay nothing plainer) that *in common Computation the Goodneſs or Badneſs of a Man's Choice is meaſured by the real intrinſick value of the thing he chuſes* ; ſo that if a Man chuſes that which is *really* and *intrinſically the worſt*,

worſt, let it be done never ſo *carefully*, it will ſtill be the *worſt Choice* ; as on the other hand, if he chuſes that which is *really* and *intrinſically the beſt*, let it be done never ſo *careleſly*, it will be the *beſt Choice*. In the Inſtance that I made uſe of to il-luſtrate this by, the Caſe was ſo clear that Mr. *Pyle* could not deny it Who makes the *beſt Choice* ? He that chuſes *Silver*, or he that chuſes *Gold* ? Mr *Pyle* owns, he that chuſes the *latter*. And who makes the *worſt Choice* ? He who chuſes the *Communion* of the *Papiſts*, or he who chuſes the *Communion* of the *Proteſtants* ? Does not he who chuſes the Communion of the *Papiſts* ? Why no (according to the Biſhop and Mr. *Pyle*) not unleſs he chuſes it *Raſhly* and *In-conſiderately*. But I ſay, *yes* ; for this Conſidera-tion has no place in the *former* Inſtance, and therefore it can have none in the *latter*. O but ſays Mr *Pyle*, (w) This is *drawing Parallels be-tween things the moſt unparallel of any things in Na-ture* ; *it is drawing down the Excellency of Moral Vertue, to the Level of that which is in Gold and Silver* ; and this he is pleaſed to obſerve as an In-ſtance of my *little Wit*, and *great Inattention* ! Mr. *Pyle* is welcome to be as Complaiſant as he pleaſes ; but let him not think that this odious Imputation upon me will paſs for an Anſwer For it is plain to any one who has but Eyes in his Head, that the *Compariſon* here made is not between the *Excellency* of *Moral Vertue*, and the *Excellency* of *Gold* and *Silver* ; but between the *Uſe* and *Signification* of theſe words, *the Beſt*, or *the worſt Choice*, when applyed to the one, and when applyed to the other. What I ſay, and what Mr *Pyle* allows, is, that in chuſing *Gold* or

---

(w) Ibid *p.* 16.

Silver,

Silver, he is always said to make the *worst Choice*, who chuses the *worst Metal*; whether he chuses it *rashly*, or *not rashly*. In like manner in chusing *Communions*; Does not he make the *worst Choice*, who chuses the *worst Communion*, whether *Rashly*, or *not Rashly*? I say, he *does*; the Bishop and Mr. *Pyle* say he does *not*. But let either of them assign a Reason for it when they can.

I know not how to forgive my self, Reader, that I have detained you so long upon such mere Trifles. But I had a mind to show you how obstinately this Author insists upon Trifles, when he wants something material to say. The Sense of the *Committee* is as clear as the Light, *viz.* That if a Man chuses the *worst Communion possible*, the Sincerity of his private Judgment will justify him. Now since this is the very Doctrine of his Lordship, what can be more plain than that he *owns* that which they have *really charged* him with, and *denys* only *that* which they have *not* To argue as Mr. *Pyle* does, that this cannot be the Sense of the *Committee*, because (*x*) it cannot be *truly affirmed* that the Sincerity of a Man's private Judgment will *not* justify him in his Choice, is ridiculous; at least *in him*. For he, I suppose, is none of those who pretend that *all* that the *Committee* have affirmed is *true*. Besides, if it be rightly understood, I think it *may be* truly affirmed, that the Sincerity of a Man's private Judgment will *not* justify him in a *bad* Choice For if you take *Justification* in a *Gospel Sense* (and in that Sense surely it ought to be taken in this Controversy) *i. e.* as it signifies Justification *according to* the *Terms* and *Conditions* laid down in the

_____

(*x*) Ibid. *p.* 15.

Gospel;

Gofpel ; *mere* Sincerity will not then juftify him *at all*. And take it how you will, it will not (as the *Committee* exprefs themfelves a few Lines after) *wholly juftify* him, *i e·* it will not *fo far* juftify him, as that it fhall be *the fame thing* to him as if he had made the *beft Choice* ———But this will be more properly fpoken to in another place; and therefore I fhall now conclude this Point with begging leave to recall one thing which I have faid in my *Remarks* under this Head. I there lay it down in effect, that according to the Bifhop's Notion of *Beft* and *Worft*, he *muft have fuppofed that by the* WORST *Choice the* Committee *meant the Choice of that which appears to a Man's own Judgment to be the worft*; in which *Suppofition*, I fay, there is *no Senfe*. Here Mr. *Pyle* is pleafed to *laugh*; as if I had *refolved all into the good Nature and Opinion of the Friends on both fides*, and he may laugh on, if he pleafes; for I only fuppofed that the *Committee* were Mafters of juft fo much common Senfe, as to know the difference between two *Contradictories*, and confequently that fince in the Cafe of chufing Communions, his Lordfhip had fo *conftantly*, and fo *plainly* taught, that a Man ought to chufe that which he *thinks* to be *the beft*; it could never be their Intention to charge him with faying, that he ought to chufe that which he *thinks* to be *the worft*. This I fay is all that I fuppofed in that Argument; and if Mr. *Pyle* will not grant me this, his *good Nature* will, I believe, be the leaft thing in Queftion But the Obfervation which Mr. *Pyle* might have made, and which he ought to have made, is this, That fince according to the Bifhop a Man does then and then only make the *beft Choice*, when he chufes that which *upon the ftricteft* and *moft impartial Enquiry* appears to him to be the beft, there was therefore, in order

der to make the Charge of the *Committee* to *con-tradict* what his Lordship *says* he maintains, no need to suppose any thing more than this, *viz.* That by the *worst Choice* the *Committee* meant the Choice of that, which tho' indeed it *appears* to be the *best*, yet it appears so only for want of *sufficient Examination.* Whether the *Committee* had Reason to suspect that this was his Lordship's Doctrine, or whether they had not, is another Question. But that they intended not in this place to *charge* him with this Doctrine, is very plain, because, as I have, I hope, sufficiently shown, the word *Worst* (upon which the whole Stress of the Charge lyes) according to the Rule of Speaking in all like Cases, relates *not* to the *Examination* which is *previous* to a Man's *Choice*, but *wholly* and *solely* to the *nature*, and *real value* of the *thing* he *chuses*

From what I have now observed concerning my own Mistake, Mr. *Pyle* may learn that I am not so hard to be perswaded to *own my self in the Wrong*, as he somewhere seems to suppose. He may also find that I am not yet reduced to such Streights, but that I can afford to lend him a helping Hand (if it be to give him a just Advantage) even against my self. Whether Mr *Pyle* will thank me for this, or whether he will not, I am willing to leave entirely to his Discretion; tho' I fancy beforehand that he will not be very well pleased to find himself under a *Mischance*, which is usually look'd upon either as a sign of *great Haste*, or *very little Judgment*; I mean the unhappiness of *spying many* Faults where there are *none*, and of *overlooking* them where *they are.*

To proceed, the next *Consequence* mentioned by me as charged upon his Lordship by the *Committee*, is, That he hath *render'd all Church Com-*
H   *munion*

munion unneceffary in order to entitle Men to the *Favour of God* Againſt this his Lordſhip has excepted nothing but this, that this *latter* part of the Charge is inconſiſtent with the *former,* wherein it is declared to be the Conſequence of his Lordſhip's Doctrine, that a Man's Private Judgment *will juſtify him, even in the worſt Choice he can make* , which, ſays his Lordſhip, *ſuppoſes* that I have *made Communion with ſome Church or other neceſſary* This I look'd upon to be an *extraordinary* Inſtance of his Lordſhip's *Artful* and *Evaſive* way of Writing ; for it being (as I have obſerved) ſo manifeſtly conſiſtent, to ſay that a Man's Private Judgment will juſtify him if he chuſes the *Worſt* Communion ; and alſo that it will juſtify him if he chuſes *no* Communion ; it being likewiſe ſo natural an Inference, that if a Man's Private Judgment will juſtify him in chuſing *no* Communion, it will juſtify him in chuſing *any* Communion · This I ſay, being ſo clearly the Caſe, I thought it impoſſible that his Lordſhip ſhould lay hold of ſo weak a Pretence as this, unleſs it were that otherwiſe he muſt have been forced to do, what yet he was reſolved *not* to do, that is, to make a plain acknowledgment of the thing laid to his Charge. Upon this Mr *Pyle* has given us an Harrangue of about two Pages long ; by which, if his Meaning was to juſtify the Biſhop againſt the *Committee,* he is ſurely the moſt unfortunate *Advocate* that ever took Cauſe in Hand, for he has given him up as *contentedly* as may be He propounds my Queſtion fairly enough, thus, *Where and how is it ſuppoſed that his Lordſhip hath made Communion with ſome Church or other neceſſary ?* And now, pray mark his Anſwer,

(y) It

(*y*) In (*i e* Communion with fome Church or other) *is* NOT *nor need be any where* SUPPOSED *as abfolutely or indifpenfably neceffary to* ALL *Men under* ALL *Circumftances* ——'Tis needlefs to repeat any thing farther; for here is a plain Conceffion, that according to his Lordfhip, the joyning in Communion with ANY Church may NOT, to SOME Perfons under SOME Circumftances, be NECESSARY *to entitle them to God's Favour* Now who thefe *Perfons*, and what thefe *Circumftances* are, you will underftand from his Anfwer to another Queftion of mine, which follows prefently after. *May not the fame Perfon,* (i e the fame Perfon who affirms that the Sincerity of a Man's Private Judgment will juftify him if he chufes the *worft* Communion ; may not, fay I, the fame Perfon) *affirm alfo very confiftently, that the fame Sincerity will likewife juftify him if he chufes none at all ?* YES, fays Mr *Pyle*, MOST CERTAINLY, *if he finds none that his Confcience and Sincere Judgment will fuffer him to efteem fit to be joyned with ; which was the only poffible Cafe wherein the Bifhop can be concluded to have juftifyed fuch a Man.* The *only poffible* Cafe, do you fay, Sir ? I fancy not. But fuppofing that it were, I think you have here very fully acknowledged the Charge of the *Committee* to be juft For when the *Committee* fay, that his Lordfhip hath *rendered all Church Communion unneceffary to entitle Men to the Favour of God,* their meaning is *not,* that he has made it (*z*) *in all Cafes, and to every Man abfolutely and equally unneceffary,* as you very extravagantly fuppofe ; but that he has made it neceffary *no further* than a Man's *Private Perfwafion* leads him

---

(*y*) Ibid, *p*. 17, 18.   (*z*) Ibid. *p*. 18.

to *think it* neceffary, fo that if his Private Judgment leads him to think it *not* neceffary to joyn himfelf in any Communion, and accordingly he *does not* joyn himfelf to any Communion, his Title to God's Favour fhall be *the fame* as if he did. This is plainly the Cafe, as will appear by confidering both parts of the Sentence together. *All Church Communion is render'd unneceffary to Entitle Men to God's Favour; and every Man is referred in thefe Cafes to his Private Judgment, as that which will juftify the worft Choice he can make* All Church Communion is rendered unneceffary —— How fo ? Why by *referring every Man to his Private Judgment*, which as it will juftify him, if he chufes the *worft* Communion, fo confequently it will alfo juftify him if he chufes *none at all*. A Man's *Private Judgment* is fuppofed to *direct* him in both Cafes, and confequently Church Communion is not here fuppofed to be made unneceffary *any farther* than *according to* that *Private Judgment* it *appears* to be unneceffary. Now, Sir, Forafmuch as you have laid it down, as your own and the Bifhop's Opinion, that a Man's Private Perfwafion will Juftify him, or Entitle him to God's Favour, tho' he chufes *no* Communion, provided, or upon this Condition that his *Confcience will not fuffer* him to *think*, that there are any *fit* to be joyned with, by this, I fay, you have plainly given up the thing in Queftion For if this be the Cafe, 'tis manifeft that there can be no neceffary Connexion between a Man's *joyning himfelf to any Communion*, and his being *Entitled to God's Favour* ; No ; his Title to God's Favour depends upon his *Private Perfwafion*, and upon *nothing elfe*. Now if a Man's *Title* to God's Favour depends *folely* upon his *Private* Perfwafion, it will follow, that the

joyning

joyning in any Communion cannot be *necessary* in order to the Entitling him to God's Favour, *any farther* than a Man's *Private Perswasion* leads him to *think* it *necessary,* which, I say, is the very Consequence charged upon his Lordship by the *Committee.* And whereas you say, that the *only possible* Case wherein the Bishop can be concluded to have justifyed a Man in chusing no Communion at all, is when his Conscience will not suffer him to esteem any FIT to be joyned with; in this I think you are widely mistaken For a Man may chuse to joyn in *no* Communion, as well because he thinks it *not necessary* to joyn in any, as because he thinks it *not fitting.* That his Private Judgment will justify him in the *latter* Case, you grant; and why it should not as well justify him in the *former,* you may be pleased to take your own Time to consider.

Whether, or in what Sense, a Man's Private Perswasion will Entitle him to God's Favour, tho' he joyns himself to *no* Communion of Christians, is a Subject proper to be considered in another place. The question at present only is, whether his Lordship is rightly charged with this Consequence ? which since he is now acknowledged to be, I think I need not be afraid to say again, as I once before said in my *Remarks,* (p 11.) That according to his Lordship, *a Man who joyns himself with* NO *Society of Christians, who frequents* NO *Place of Publick Worship, who partakes of* NO *Sacraments, may yet have a Title to God's Favour, and that in the same Degree with him who sincerely keeps the whole Law.* I observed there indeed, that his Lordship had said one thing, which, were it true, would take off this Objection: But then I observed likewise, that it would make his whole Doctrine about Sincerity *insignificant.*

(a) *Hard,*

(a) *Hard*, fays Mr *Pyle, that the Objection should be removed, and yet the Doctrine be destroyed!* An Obfervation fo very *thin* and *flippery*, that he no fooner lays hold of it than he *lets it go again*, and comes to the Bifhop's *Suppofition,* which I faid was this; That *thofe who fincerely believe in Chrift, will be led by their Regard to him to the Profeffion of that Truth, and to the outward Ufe of* ALL *the* MEANS *which he appointed,* i e as I have explained it, they will be led by their Regard to Chrift, to *believe* and *do* as the Gofpel directs them This I farther confirmed from another Paffage, in which his Lordfhip had declared, that *it* CANNOT BE SUPPOSED, *that a Man who fincerely is Subject to Jefus Chrift alone in the great Affair of Salvation, will not follow Jefus Chrift's Directions, and join in the Worfhip of God with other Men, or will not be induced to follow* ALL *his Mafter's* INJUNCTIONS This is his Lordfhip's *Suppofition,* which afterwards he applys particularly to the Cafe of the *Sacraments* ; and, which I fay, if it be true (which I have fhewn it not to be) takes off the Objection For if the only thing which can Entitle a Man to God's Favour, notwithftanding he joyns himfelf to no Communion of Chriftians, be his *Sincerity* , and if *it cannot be fuppofed,* that a Man who is Sincere, *may* refufe to joyn himfelf to any Communion of Chriftians. becaufe all who are fincere *muft* be led to follow *all* the *Injunctions,* or *Appointments* of Chrift Then indeed, it will not follow from any thing that his Lordfhip hath faid, That a Man who joyns in *no* Communion, or even in a *wrong* Communion,

(*a*) Ibid. *p.* 19.

wil

will have as good a Title to God's Favour, as he who joyns in a *Right* one But then on the other hand, his Lordship will be made to have said a great deal to very little Purpose. For how idle is it, to tell us, that *Sincerity* will justify a Man *if he be* in an Error, *i e. if* he does *not* follow all Chrift's Injunctions, if it be true, that Sincerity *cannot be suppofed, unlefs* a Man *does* follow all Chrift's Injunctions?

This is the State of the Cafe ; and now let us attend a little upon Mr. *Pyle,* and fee how he has endeavoured to bring the Bishop off. He grants then, that *as I have quoted thefe two Expreffions (Sentences,* I fuppofe he would have faid*) and remarked upon them, a Reader would indeed naturally think, his Lordship had not only fuppofed, but affirmed, that* ALL *fincere Chriftians*———*muft of courfe be led to*———*an uniform Reception of* ALL *the Doctrines, and appointed Means of* Chrift, *as they were defigned to be underftood in the Gofpel Writings.* Which Words I no fooner read, than I began vehemently to fufpect that here was more *Trumping* at hand ; and fo indeed it proved. For in the next Page he tells me, that this is *a grofs Mifreprefentation* That *all this Hacking, and Hewing down of the Bifhop's Principle, is merely in* my own *Brain, by either defignedly, or very unfortunately taking a thing to be affirmed by one, which was only by Confequence, and on bare Suppofition the Affirmation of the other* Certainly this Gentleman cares not what he fays! For tho' I do not pretend to make either Senfe *Grammar* of this Sentence, yet the meaning of it (if Mr *Pyle*'s Intention was to contradict me) muft be this That whereas I have fet it down as a *Suppofition,* or an *Affertion* (for you may call it which you pleafe) of *the Bifhop's,* that all fincere Chriftians *will,* and *muft,* by their Regard

gard to Chrift be led to follow *all* his *Injunctions*; this is NOT *the Bifhop's* Suppofition, BUT *the Committee's*, 1 e. (I fuppofe) that the Bifhop *fpoke this*, not *as his own*, but *as the Committee's* Suppofition; for every one fees that the Paffages upon which I ground this Obfervation, are quoted, *not* out of the *Reprefentation*, *but* out of the *Bifhop's Anfwer*. Now if this be indeed the Cafe, I will be contented to be thought either as *Defigning*, or as *unfortunate* a Man as Mr. *Pyle* is difpofed to think me to be; but furely it is impoffible that any thing can be more notoriously falfe! For, pray obferve. The Bifhop, as I faid in my *Remarks*, had defined *the Church* to be *the Number of Men, whether fmall or great, difperfed, or united, who truly and fincerely are Subjects to* Jefus Chrift *alone as their Lawgiver and Judge*, &c. The *Committee* upon this, charged him with having contradicted the 19th *Article* of our *Church*, in which it is defined to be *a Congregation of faithful Men, in which the pure Word of God is Preached, and the Sacraments duly Adminiftred*, &c. The Bifhop replies, that whereas the *Article* defines the *vifible* Church of Chrift, he had defined the *Invifible* one; acknowledging at the fame, that if in his Definition of this *latter*, it could be proved that any thing was contained which contradicted *that Definition* which the *Article* has given of the *former*, it would be his part to anfwer for it His Bufinefs therefore was to fhow that there was *no fuch* Contradiction; and thus he attempts it. *Can it be thought by this Learned Body, that a Man's being of the Invifible Church, is inconfiftent with his joyning himfelf with any Vifible Church? That a Man who fincerely is Subject to* Jefus Chrift *alone, in the great Affair of Salvation*, WILL NOT *follow* Jefus Chrift's *Directions, and joyn*

11

in the Worship of God with other Men ; or will not be induced to follow ALL *his Master's Injunctions ? If therefore the main and principal Foundation of what I have taught ; the Description which I have given of the Church, do not either in Words, or in Consequence contradict the* Article *of our Church here mentioned, it is impossible to suppose, that I should intend any of my Observations upon this Subject, by way of Disparagement, &c.* Answ. *to the* Repres. Chap 1. Sect. 14 p 79

Thus argues the Bishop ; whether Pertinently, or not Pertinently, it matters not now to enquire. That which at present lies before us, is this, and only this, whether it be *his Lordship's,* or the *Committee's* Supposition, that a Man who is sincerely Subject to Jesus Christ, *will,* and *must* be led to follow *all* Jesus Christ's Injunctions ? and I think, for my part, that the Case is as clear as can be For, 1. This Question, CAN IT BE *supposed by this Learned Body* amounts in plain and necessary Construction to a *positive Assertion,* that IT CANNOT BE *supposed by this Learned Body.* Consequently hisLordship does not in these words refer to any thing, which *had been* supposed by the *Committee ;* he only tells them what they *ought,* or *ought not* to suppose. 2. *One* of those things which the Bishop says the *Committee* CANNOT *suppose,* is, *that a Man who is a sincere Subject of Jesus* Christ, WILL NOT *be induced to follow* ALL *his Injunctions.* Now if the *Committee* cannot suppose this, the Reason must be, because *in the nature of the thing* IT CANNOT BE supposed ; for if it MAY at all be supposed, then *the Committee* may suppose it, unless you think that *the Committee* are under an Obligation to suppose nothing but what the Bishop has a mind to. This then is a plain Declaration *on the Bishop's side,* that it MUST BE supposed that EVERY sincere Subject of Jesus Christ WILL be

I   led

led to follow ALL Jesus Christ's Injunctions;
which will, if it be possible, be the more manifest from what follows in the next Section. He
there declares once more (in Answer to the *Committee*, who had blamed him for leaving out
Preaching the Word, and *Administring* the *Sacra-
men.* in his Definition of the Church) that he
was not speaking of a *Visible* Church, but of the
Invisible Church, *made up of such as sincerely believe in Christ, and* BY CONSEQUENCE WILL BE LED
*by their Regard to him, both to the Profession of that
Faith, and to the outward Use of* ALL *the Means
which he has appointed* Is not this a plain Declaration *in the Bishop's Name,* that ALL sincere
Believers WILL be led, *in Vertue of their Sincerity* merely, *to the Use of* ALL *the Means appointed by
Christ* If you doubt, read the next Words: *To
make such Objections as these, is to make Objections
that have no Weight in them, unless they who make
them suppose, that by taking* Christ *for their Lawgiver and King, Men will not be led by him and his
own Directions, to the* TWO SACRAMENTS, *and to the
Use of his own* APPOINTMENTS : *A* SUPPOSITION
which I SHALL TAKE CARE *never to be guilty of*
Mr. *Pyle* in relating this Passage, has intirely
dropt these last words, *a Supposition which I shall
take care,* &c. thro' *Bashfulness,* it may be, not
caring to be stared so full in the Face. For in
the very next line he was to call upon his Friend,
*to see whose this Supposition was, that is, to destroy
his Lordship's darling Scheme* ; meaning to bid
him look if it was not *the Committee's* ; which
would have been a very bold Challenge, if these
last Words had been set down, which do so manifestly show it to be the *Bishop's* Indeed, that it
should be a Supposition of *the Committee,* that e-
very sincere Man, will, *in Vertue of his Sincerity only,
be led to follow* ALL Christ's *Injunctions,* is a Con-
ceit

ceit every whit as extravagant, as the Reason which appears to have given birth to this Observation, is Abſurd and Ridiculous Mr *Pyle* having ſtated the *Committee's* Objection, ſets down the Biſhop's Anſwer, thus; *That there could be no Inconſiſtency between the two Definitions, unleſs it could be ſuppoſed* BY THAT LEARNED BODY *(for,* adds he, *'twas* THEIRS, *not my* LORD'S *Suppoſition) That a Man who is ſincerely Subject to* Jeſus Chriſt, *will* NOT *follow,* &c Judge now, Reader, if this which I am going to tell you was not the Caſe. Mr. *Pyle* had very happily found out, that theſe words, *Suppoſed, by, that, Learned, Body,* ſtood cloſe together in the Biſhop's Book Preſently up ſtarts a Thought in his Head, that his Lordſhip here was not declaring any thing *as his own Suppoſition,* but only mentioning ſomething which had been ſuppoſed *by the Committee* Now if this ſhould happen to be that very *Suppoſition* which I had charged upon his Lordſhip, as *Deſtructive of his darling Scheme,* what a clever Diſcovery would this be ! What Triumphs might be raiſed ! ——— Well, thus then it muſt be ; and accordingly no ſooner had he made an end of ſetting down the Biſhop's Anſwer, but out it comes at a Venture, that this *Deſtruction* is all *Imaginary,* all *Framed in my own Brain,* by making that to be a Suppoſition *of the one,* which in Truth was a Suppoſition of *the other* But as haſty Projects ſeldom proſper, eſpecially where the Intention is not good, ſo it hath happen'd even in this Caſe ; for if any Regard is o be paid to Mr *Pyle's* own *Words,* this *Suppoſition,* which he ſays was theirs (the Committee's) and not *his Lordſhip's,* is not *that Suppoſition* which I *have charged* upon his Lordſhip, and which I ſay *deſtroys his*

I 2   *darling*

darling Scheme, but the *direct contrary* to it. *That Supposition* which *I have charged* upon his Lordship, is, (as you have seen over and over) *that a sincere Subject* of Jesus Christ WILL *be led to follow all* Jesus Christ's *Injunctions.* Whereas the Supposition which Mr. *Pyle* says is *the Committee's*, and not *his Lordship's*, is (as you'll perceive by reading the Passage) *not that a sincere Subject of* Jesus Christ WILL *be led*, but *that he* WILL NOT *be led to follow all* Jesus Christ's *Injunctions.* Mr. *Pyle*, on account of some gross and enormous Mistakes, which, as he fancies, I have committed, has often told me of my BLUNDERS, and Complemented me with a Variety of such Terms, as I must own are by much *too good* to be returned him back again. But this I do assure him, that as great a *Blunderer* as I am, I have still such a Sense of what is *Just* and *Decent*, that I will never again trouble the World with my *Writings*, when once the Case comes to be so bad with me, that I cannot see *to what* a plain Sentence in any Author *refers*, or at least am not able to know the difference between a *Negative* and an *Affirmative*

But to proceed ; It appearing so plainly to be *his Lordship's* Supposition, *that a sincere Subject* of Jesus Christ *will be led by his Regard to* Christ, *to the Profession of that Faith, and to the outward Use of* ALL *the Means which he appointed* ; *or be induced to follow* ALL *his Master's Injunctions*; our next enquiry must be, what may be *the Sense* of this Supposition The Sense which I have put upon it, is very well expressed by Mr. *Pyle*, VIZ. That ALL *sincere Christians must of course be led to an uniform Reception of* ALL *the Doctrines and appointed Means of Christ, as they were designed to be understood in the Gospel.* Now to this he says,
1. That

1. That *it is a false and a groundless Suppofition* By which, if he means that the Suppofition *it felf*, when underftood in this Senfe, is falfe and groundlefs, I agree with him. He fays, 2 That it is *the Refult of nothing but of a moft unfair Reprefentation of the Bifhop's Words*; by which, if he means that my putting this Senfe upon the Bifhop's Suppofition, is the Refult of nothing but of a moft unfair Reprefentation of the Bifhop's Words, I fhall difpute it with him. Let us hear then how Mr. *Pyle* interprets thefe Words. *Sincere Believers in* Chrift *will be led to that Faith, and to all the Means which he has appointed.* That is, fays he, *They will be led to the Profeffion of all that Faith, and to the Ufe of all thofe Means which their honeft Endeavours will enable them to attain to*——*Again ; They will follow all* Chrift's *Directions, i e to the beft of their Knowledge.*——*And joyn in the Worfhip of God with other Men, i. e. with all, or any Men whom they judge to Worfhip God aright, and with none any farther.* This Mr. *Pyle* fays is *the candid Senfe,* and *natural Intention* of thefe Expreffions ; and that fo plainly, that (had not I, it feems, by my Example fhown the contrary) he *fhould verily have thought that ill Nature it felf could have hardly gone fo far as to deny it.* Concerning Mr. *Pyle's good Nature* I have nothing to fay. But I fhall mightily queftion his *good Senfe,* if he can in earneft believe that his Lordfhip's Meaning was as he has now defcribed it to be. For, 1. He (Mr *Pyle*) himfelf has given us *another* Senfe of thefe Expreffions, which is not at all agreeable with this. The *Committee,* fays the Bifhop, *cannot fuppofe that a Man who is a fincere Subject of* Jefus Chrift, WILL NOT (*i. e* fays Mr. *Pyle,* CANNOT CONSISTENTLY *be fuppofed to*) *follow*

follow all his Injunctions Again, *The Committee cannot suppose, that by taking* Christ *for their Lawgiver, and King,* Men WILL NOT (*i. e* says he, CANNOT CONSISTENTLY) *be led to the use of his own Appointments,* and particularly *to the Sacraments* In both these Instances you see Mr *Pyle* interprets the words WILL NOT, by CANNOT CONSISTENTLY, that is, WILL is made to signify MAY, or CAN ; and so by the same Rule *Black* may be made to signify *White*, *Red*, *Yellow* ; *any* thing, *every* thing. Thus, I say, may the Sense of Words be turned toply turvy, *i e.* when Mr. *Pyle thinks so fit,* and it will *suit with his Purpose* ; for I believe, were I to give him a *Note* under my Hand, wherein I promised that *I would* pay him a *Hundred Pounds* upon Demand, he would hardly be so *good natured* as to think my Meaning to be no more than, that I *might consistently* do it ——But this by the way. That which I principally observe here is this, That this Interpretation and the former, cannot both of them be right For if by *will not*, his Lordship means *cannot consistently*, then by *following all Chrift's Injunctions* or *Appointments*, he could not mean barely following them (as Mr. *Pyle* supposes) *according to the best of his Judgment*, or *Abilities*; because there can be no doubt, but that a sincere Man *may consistently* with his Sincerity be led to follow Chrift's Appointments, not only *according to the best of his Judgment*, but *actually*, or according to that Sense wherein they are set down, and *designed to be understood* in the Gospel To say the Truth, *Sincerity* in a Christian (according to his Lordship, at least) implies in the very Notion of it the following all the Injunctions, or Appointments of Chrift, *according to the best of a Man's Abilities.* To say there-

therefore that a sincere Subject of Jesus Christ
will, 1 e. *consistently may* follow all the Injunctions or Appointments of Christ, according to
the best of his Abilities, is only to say, that a
sincere Christian *may consistently be* a sincere Christian; a Discovery, which how worthy soever
it may be of Mr *Pyle*, is such as I am sure his
Lordship would be heartily ashamed of For
this Reason 2. It could not be his Lordship's
Intention to say, that a sincere Subject of Jesus
Christ WILL follow all the Injunctions, or Appointments of Christ *according to the best of his*
Abilities; for this would amount only to this
Identical Proposition, that a sincere Christian
will be a sincere Christian. And 3. There is a-
nother Reason to be given why this could not
be his Meaning, *viz* That his Lordship hath
expresly specified the *Two Sacraments*, and *Ex-*
ternal Communion, as of the Number of those *Ap-*
pointments of Christ, which he says, every sincere
Subject of Christ will by his Regard to Christ be
led to follow. Consequently therefore by *Ap-*
pointments his Lordship could not mean (as according to Mr. *Pyle*, he must be supposed to
have meant) Such things as to a sincere Man,
appear to be Appointments, but such as *really are*
so, for *such* are the *Two Sacraments*, and *Exter-*
nal Communion. And there is no Sense, in saying that a sincere Christian will joyn *in the Use*
of the Sacraments, according to the best of his
Abilities; tho' it were Sense to say *in General*,
that he will follow *all the Injunctions of Christ*,
according to the best of his Abilities For
ought I can see therefore, Mr *Pyle* must be contented to lay aside *the best of his Abilities*, and
stand wholly to the other Interpretation, to wit,
That a sincere Christian *may consistently* be led to
all

all the Injunctions of Chrift, *i e.* as they are
fet down in the Gofpel This will be a *weighty*
Propofition too ; but (which is as muchas can
be expected) it may be underftood, that is,
(*N B.*) if you will give Mr *Pyle* the liberty of making the Words, *Will,* and *May,* fignify the fame thing But not to infift any longer upon this, I fhall make one Obfervation
more, which will effectually overthrow both thefe
Interpretations at once, *viz* 4. That the Nature of the Argument requires that his Lordfhip's Words be underftood in that Senfe which
I have put upon them, and which Mr. *Pyle* re-
jects, *i. e* as fignifying, That *all* fincere Chriftians will be led to *an uniform Reception* of ALL
the *Doctrines,* and *appointed Means* of Chrift, *as
they were defigned to be underftood in the Gofpel.*
For, pray obferve. The Queftion between his
Lordfhip and the *Committee* was, whether *his*
Definition of the *Church* did not contradict the
Definition given in the 19th *Article* The Com-
mittee faid *it did,* becaufe the *Article* had made
the Preaching of the Word, and *the Adminiftration
of the Sacraments according to Chrift's Appointment,*
effential to the Notion of the Church, which his
Lordfhip's Definition had *not.* In Anfwer to
this, his Lordfhip obferves, 1 That according
to him the Church confifted of thofe who are
fincerely Subject to Jefus Chrift, as their King
and Lawgiver 2 That *all fuch Perfons* would
be led by their Regard to Chrift to follow *all
his Injunctions* and *Appointments,* and confequently to *join in the Worfhip* of God *with other Men,
and partake of the Sacraments.* If his Lordfhip
did not hereby intend to fhow, that the *Preaching
of the Word,* and the *Ufe of the Sacraments* were,
tho' not *expreffed in,* yet *implyed under* his Definition,

nition, I will venture to say, that he intended nothing but to impose upon his Readers. And if *he did* intend this, 'tis plain that when he says, that *all* the sincere Subjects of Jesus Christ will be led to follow *all* Jesus Christ's Injunctions, his Meaning must be, that they will *actually fulfil* whatever Jesus Christ has *Enjoyned,* or *Commanded* in the Gospel. For if it be only true, that such Persons *may confistently* fulfil *all* that is commanded in the Gospel, it will also be true, that *confistently* they *may not* do it. Or if it be only true, that such Persons *will, according to the best of their Abilities,* fulfil *all* that is commanded in the Gospel, it will also be true, that *for want of Abilities,* they *may possibly fail in many Particulars* Neither of these Suppositions therefore will afford Foundation for any just Inference, that *all* sincere Subjects of Jesus Christ will be led *to joyn in the Publick Worship of God with other Men,* and *to the Use of the Sacraments;* and consequently upon neither of them will the *Preaching of the Word,* and *Administring the Sacraments,* be included under his Lordship's Definition.

It appears then in spite of all Mr. *Pyle's* Cavilling, that the Bishop *has supposed,* and *asserted,* that *all* Sincere Christians *will* be led to an *uniform Reception of* ALL *the Doctrines and Injunctions of the Gospel.* Not that this was his Lordship's real Opinion, no, but he said it merely because it was necessary to serve a present Purpose ; and hereby he has given us such an Instance of disingenuous Dealing, as it were to be wished might be forgotten, and
K. which

which therefore I am sorry that Mr. *Pyle* has given me this Occasion to repeat The Case, as I have stated it in my *Remarks*, is plainly this, That if his Lordship had not asserted this, he must have said, that a Man *may be* a Member of HIS *Invisible Church*, tho' he be not a Member of the *Visible One*; i. e he may be a *true Member of Christ's Church* (for *such*, I suppose, his Lordship conceives *all* the Members of HIS *Invisible Church* to be) and in consequence hereof entitled to *all* the Benefits and Priviledges of the Gospel, tho' he partakes of *no Sacrament*, nor by any other Act becomes *joyned in Visible Communion* with other Christians. This Consequence Mr *Pyle* owns, and justifies; for he says, that (*b*) *The Omission of* NO *External Means can exclude a Man from Membership in the Invisible Church, if he be sincerely perswaded that the External Usages of* [all] *the Visible Communities he knows of are not Obligatory.* Frankly spoken indeed! But the Bishop foresaw, and has in effect *confessed*, that had *he* said thus much, he must at the same time have justified the *Committee.* To *make such Objections as these,* says he, *is to make Objections that have no Weight in them,* UNLESS *they who make them suppose, that by taking* Christ *for their King,* Men WILL NOT *be led to the Two Sacraments, and to the Use of his own Appointments* What *these Objections* were, you have heard often enough; and you now hear his Lordship himself acknowledging in effect,

---

(*b*) Ibid. p. 23.

that

that if what he here mentions can be *supposed*, these Objections will be *of Weight*. His Lordship then, I will venture to fay, knows in his own Conscience that this *may be* supposed ; he knows, or will not *deny* at least, that there are Multitudes of those who *take Christ for their King*, who *are* not *led to the Two Sacraments* ; and his Doctrine about *Sincerity*, either labours under the Absurdity of providing against a Case that can never happen, or else *it must* suppose, that *to take Christ for ones King*, and yet not to *follow all his Appointments*, are very consistent things. His Lordship therefore is plainly *Self-condemned* ; and as to Mr *Pyle*, how *honest* a part soever he may have acted in thus freely declaring his Opinion, he has certainly acted a very *unfortunate* one, in granting *that* which, even in the Sense of the Bishop *himself*, leaves him open to the Justice of that Charge, against which he has spent so many Words in endeavouring to defend him.

What is the true Scriptural Notion of the Word Church, as it was never a Point between his Lordship and the *Committee*, so I will take care it shall be none between Mr. *Pyle* and me. The *Committee supposed* that it was what the 19th *Article* made it to be, and I do think it will be by no means proper for me to enter into any Debate *with that Gentleman*, whether this *Article* be *right*, or whether it be *wrong*. To proceed therefore, The *last* Consequence charged by me upon his Lordship's Doctrine, is, that according to it *the Religion of* Jesus Christ *in the largest Sense*

of

of the Word, or as it takes in all those who believe in Jesus Christ, is of no greater Efficacy
towards procuring God's Favour, than the Religion of Mahomet. This Consequence was
mentioned by me, as *added to those* which
had been drawn by the Committee; *by which,*
says (c) Mr. *Pyle, I suppose we are to understand
it to be his own; tho',* adds he, *the Words show
us he has done herein nothing but borrowed from
M. Law ,* or (as he has it in the next Page,
and elsewhere very frequently) HIS MASTER
Law If Mr *Pyle* had intended this as a
Compliment, I should have thanked him; but
since I perceive 'tis designed as a *Reflection*
upon the *Master,* and the *Disciple* both; I
can only tell him that he has missed his End.
I think it no Reproach to me, Sir, to be
taught by Mr. *Law ,* no, not even by *your
self,* when you'll be pleased to favour us with
any thing that is worth the learning But
since I am thus called upon by Mr *Pyle,* to
give an Account where I had this Observation, I can tell him with a very safe Conscience, that I had it *not* from Mr *Law,* whose
Writings I had not before me to Copy after;
tho' I must confess I had it from another
Master, whom Mr. *Pyle* seems to hold in as
great Contempt as he does Mr. *Law*; I mean
common Sense, which without sending me to
turn over what had been said by others upon
this Subject, told me plainly, that if *all Sincere Persons* are in Vertue of their Sincerity

---

(c) Ibid. *p.* 26.

merely

merely *alike Entitled* to God's Favour, it cannot possibly signify any thing as to God's Favour, provided a Man be but *Sincere*, whether he be a *Christian*, or whether he be a *Mahometan* Now whereas Mr *Pyle* mentions it as *something beneath me and my Recommenders too*, that I had *rehearsed the Argument without the least notice of any Answers given already to it*; (meaning, *by himself*, and some others, I know not who) I am in no manner of pain for this neither For my *common Sense* also informed me that there was no occasion to trouble my self with these Answers; and Mr. *Pyle* has now fully satisfied me in what I always was apt to believe, *viz*. that these Answers, how *full and clear* soever they might *appear to his Lordship's Advocates*, were indeed nothing to the Purpose. To illustrate this Consequence which I had charged upon his Lordship's Doctrine, the more fully, I had produced that Argument which his Lordship had called a *Demonstration*, and shown that it was every whit as conclusive to justify *Mahometans* against *Christians*, as *Protestants* against *Papists* How does Mr *Pyle* answer this? How? Why, after his usual manner, so as to give up the very Point which the Argument was brought to prove! *No body denies*, says he, *but it* (the Argument) *will* (justify *Mahometans*, *Jews*, &c. against *Christians*) *in the true Sense of Sincerity and Justification*. Concerning the *true Sense* of *Sincerity*, we have no dispute : Now the *true Sense* of *Justification*, according to Mr *Pyle*, you know is this ; That all sincere Persons, without Exception shall, without any regard had

to

to the Methods of Religion, which they have feverally followed, be all *fo far juftified* and *accepted*, as to have *Rewards proportionable* to their *feveral Advancements*, or *Improvements* in *Virtuous Qualifications.* If this be true, then what I fay is true, *viz.* That according to the Bifhop, it fignifies nothing as to a Man's Title to God's Favour, whether he be a *Chriftian*, or *not a Chriftian*; for if *all* depends upon the *Sincerity* of Men, and their *Virtuous Improvements*, 'tis plain that the *Method* of *Religion*, as fuch, can make no difference. Mr. *Pyle* therefore, if he pleafes, may go on in faying, *It has been abundantly declared, that it neither was, nor poffibly could be the meaning of his Lordfhip's Pofition to mount* Mahometans, &*c to a Level in Degrees of future Rewards with* Chriftians. All I fhall be able to infer from hence, will be, that when a thing is made out never fo plainly, a Man may ftill continue to talk on, in hopes to confound his Readers by a multiplicity of words. And that this has been Mr. *Pyle*'s trne Intent and Meaning throughout this whole Debate, his Way, and Manner of Writing does, I think, too *abundantly declare.*

And now I am at laft got through a piece of Work, the moft tedious of any I ever yet undertook in my whole Life; and I queftion not but the Reader will agree with me, that if Mr. *Pyle* be fo *able* a Writer as the Bifhop has reprefented him, he never once met with a more *willing* one I cannot but fay, that I always thought this part of my Book to be of all others liable to the leaft exception; it

con-

confifting mainly of fuch plain Obfervations, as I thought no Man's common Senfe could fuffer himto differ with me about. So that when I found Mr. *Pyle* purfuing me fo clofe, and endeavouring to trip up my Heels every Step I took, I began vehemently to fufpect that fomething more than a Concern for the Truth muft be at the bottom And it feems I was not deceived ; for now at the clofe of all, the *Secret* drops out, and the meaning of all this *Worrying* is declared to be, *(d) That I may not complain for want of a Reply to any* ONE THING *upon this Head.* I do affure you, Sir, I fhould have complained *lefs* if you had replied to *fewer*; and lefs *ftill*, if you had replied to *none at all* · But *the Bifhop*, I fuppofe, would have complained, if you had failed of a Reply to *any one thing,* and therefore you were refolved to go on and juftify him in *every thing,* whether there was a Reafon for it, or whether there was none ! If Mr. *Pyle* did not mean to fay thus much, his Conduct I am fure will juftify *me* in faying it. And fince this is the Cafe, he muft not take it ill to be told, that for the future I fhall pay no particular Regard to any thing that he may think fit to Publifh againft me. *Once* to do it, I thought it *Juft* as well as *Decent* ; but as the Cafe ftands, neither *Juftice* nor *Decency* can require thatI fhould do it *more than once* If his Lordfhip is not now convinced that his Friend *deferves* no Notice, the World, I hope, is ; for certainly when once it appears that a Man will be *fatisfied with* no—

(d) Ibid. *p.* 26, 27.

thing, it is acting a reasonable and a prudent part to *give him nothing.*

The Result of the whole is this. That according to the Account which Mr. *Pyle* himself has given us of the Bishop's Opinion, it must be true what I have laid to his Charge, That *provided a Man be but Sincere, it signifies nothing what Religion he is of.* For he tells us, that those who chuse *no* Communion, or a *bad* Communion; those who partake of the *Sacraments*, and those who partake of *no Sacraments*; those who are *Christians*, and those who are *no Christians*, if they are but *Sincere*, are all of them *equally justified*, i. e. they are *in this Sense* equally justified, that the diversity of Religions, or Ways of Worship which they have followed, will not hinder them from being *all* of them *Entitled* to *Rewards proportionate* to their *Moral Improvements* This is all that ever I charged upon his Lordship; for tho' I observed (*p.* 22 of my *Remarks*) that his Lordship's Principle as he hath stated it, left no room for God in dispensing his Favours in a Life to come, to make any difference between one Man and another upon the Account of their *Moral Qualifications*; yet I never made that Point any part of the Debate, but laying it aside as that which I presumed his Lordship never intended to meddle with, confined my self all along to this single Question, *viz Whether all Sincere Persons are Entitled to an equal Share of God's Favour, notwithstanding any Difference that there is between them, with respect to the particular Method of Religion, which they each of them severally followed.*

lowed. **The** Method of Religion *as such,* was the thing concerning which the Inquiry was, whether it makes a difference or not; Mr. *Pyle* you see, says it makes *no* difference, and he says true, if it be true that *Sincerity* is the ONLY *Condition* required in the Gospel, in order to give us a *Title* to the *Rewards* of the Gospel For upon this Supposition an Honest *Heathen* has as good a Title to the Favour of God as an Honest *Christian* ; and he who lives *according to* the Gospel, shall have *no better claim* to its *Promises* than he who *Subverts* the *Faith* and *Practice* of the Gospel. Once more then I ask, is *Sincerity* the ONLY *Condition* of the Gospel, or is it not? Mr. *Pyle* (e) says *it is* ; but instead of proving it, puts us off with a Promise that he intends to prove it, *whensoever I shall make it necessary for him to do so* ; though at the same time he very well knew that I had *already* made it necessary, and left the whole of the Debate to depend upon this Issue What might be the occasion of this Backwardness in Mr. *Pyle*, he best knows, tho' I think 'tis no hard matter to guess ; but forasmuch as he has not thought fit to say any to this Point, 'tis unreasonable *in him* to expect that I should. I have already declared my Opinion on the other side, and if any thing be wanting to support it, it shall be considered in the *Defence* of the *third* part of my *Remarks*, which (unless his Lordship by any future Declarations of his Meaning shall make it unnecessary)I intend shortly to publish in a distinct Treatise.

One thing I have now to ask of his Lordship, namely, That he would be pleased to deduct one out of that *Heap* of *Contradictions* and *In-*

(e) Ibid. *p.* 36.

L.   *confi-*

confifteacies, which HE has thought fit to *lay* upon the Reverend the *Dean* of *Chichefter* The *Dean* had declared, that a *Perfwafion of Errors and Corruptions in the Eftablifh'd Church will* EXCUSE *a Separation from it.* Now *this*, fays (*f*) the Bifhop, *is that very Doctrine of* SINCERITY *which was Cenfured by the* Dean, *and his Brethren of the* Committee, *&c* But it is manifeft that a Man may be *excufed* in a Separation from the Eftablifhed Church, *i e. releafed* from any *Obligation* to Communicate with the Eftablifhed Church, without being *juftified*, i e without having any *Claim* to God's *Promifes* by the New Covenant He may be *acquitted* of the *Peaalties* of the Gofpel, and yet not *Entitled* to the *Rewards* of the Gofpel. That this is what the Dean meant by *juftifying*, is too notorious to be denied; and therefore upon this Foot, as HE will be made to fpeak confiftently with himfelf ; fo *I* may hope to avoid another Charge, which indeed equally affects us both, *viz.* the *permitting a Preface to be prefixed to my Book, in which the* Dean *grofly contradicts and ridicules the Principles of that very Treatife he profeffes to recommend.* The Doctrine which the *Dean* oppofes in this *Preface*, is this, That *Sincerity Entitles Men to* God's FAVOUR, *i e* (as he has explained himfelf) THAT *Favour which he has Publifhed, Declared, and promifed to Mankind thro' the Means provided in the Gofpel ;* contradiftinguifhed to THAT *Goodnefs and Mercy of God, which, for ought we know, he may extend beyond the Limits of the Gofpel* The Doctrine contained in *my Treatife*, is, That *nothing but Performance of the* CONDITIONS *of the Gofpel will Entitle Men to the* REWARDS *of the Gofpel, tho' they*

(*f*) *Common Rights of Subjects Defended*, &c. p. 115 117.

may

may be fure of a GOOD *Reward,* i. e of a State of Happinefs hereafter. When the Bifhop can fhow that thefe two Doctrines are *Contradictory,* he will at the fame time fhew that the *Dean* hath contradicted *me,* and not before. Tho', were he able to do it, why he fhould infinuate that my PERMITTING (as he is pleafed to fpeak) this *Preface* to be prefix'd to my Book, is an Argument of *Difingenuity* in me ; I do not underftand. His Lordfhip has of late been a great dealer in *Prefaces* and *Poftfcripts.* Mr. *Pilloniere,* and Mr *Sykes,* are both his Debtors on that Score. Whether when his Lordfhip tender'd them this *Honour,* either of them demanded a Sight of his Papers before they were Publifhed, left afterwards they fhould find themfelves *Ridicul'd,* is beft known to themfelves. But if they did, as his Lordfhip on the one hand fhew'd an uncommon Generofity to one of them, whofe Book (if I remember rightly) he ufher'd into the World, tho' as he afterwards declared he had *never once read it* ; fo *they* on the other hand did not fhew that Regard to his Lordfhip's *good Senfe,* which ENVY *her felf* will not be able to fay, I ought not to have paid to the *Dean's.*

To Conclude, if his Lordfhip's Doctrine be as I have here reprefented it, he muft not pretend to fay that I have not *differed from him one Hair's breadth.* For that all Sincere Perfons *are* Entitled to the Rewards of the Gofpel , and that all Sincere Perfons are *not* Entitled to the Rewards of the Gofpel , that Sincerity is the only Condition, or that Sincerity is *not* the *only* Condition of the New Covenant , are Propofitions as diametrically oppofite the one to the other, as Light is to Darknefs ; and confequently, if his Lordfhip maintains the *former,* it cannot

not truly be pretended that I have not *contra-dicted* him, by maintaining the *latter*. But if his Lordſhip ſhall renounce this Doctrine, and declare plainly that he intended only to ſay, that no Perſons who have uſed their conſtant Endeavours to pleaſe God, ſhall be *condemned* ; tho' he will never be able to perſwade me, that his Words imply no more, yet I ſhall rejoyce in this Happy Agreement with him in the Truth ; and ſhall think my ſelf diſengaged from all Obligation to proceed any farther in this Controverſy The Diſpute then will lie, not between his Lordſhip and *me*, but between his Lordſhip and *his Friends*, whom he has deceived into a wrong Opinion ; and I ſhall think it but juſt, that he who was the Inſtrument of *giving* the *Scandal*, ſhould alſo be the Inſtrument of *removing* it

F I N I S.

Lightning Source UK Ltd.
Milton Keynes UK
UKHW022150280720
367329UK00010B/251